WITHDRAWN

Children's Rhymes and Rhythms

Children's Counting-Out Rhymes, Fingerplays, Jump-Rope and Bounce-Ball Chants and Other Rhythms

A Comprehensive English-Language Reference

Compiled and written by

Gloria T. Delamar

McFarland 1983

Jefferson, North Carolina, and London

Library of Congress Cataloguing-in-Publication Data

Delamar, Gloria T
  Children's counting-out rhymes, fingerplays, jump-rope and bounce-ball chants and other rhythms.

  Spine title: Children's rhymes and rhythms.
  Includes index.
  1. Counting-out rhymes. 2. Jump rope rhymes.
3. Finger play. 4. Children — Folklore. I. Title.
II. Title: Children's rhymes and rhythms.
GR485.D44 1983   398'.8   82-24904

ISBN 0-89950-064-1

Manufactured in the United States of America

McFarland & Company, Inc., Publishers
  Box 611, Jefferson, North Carolina 28640

To
W.T.D.
and
"the five we love"

Acknowledgments

Most of the material in this volume has been passed from person to person in folk-tradition. Thus, the names of the original authors have been lost as the years have passed. To every *Author unknown*, I owe a debt of appreciation. Every effort has been made to find the authors of the work included here. Any lack of copyright information or credit omission is unintentional. Where the authors have been known, credit has been given.

No acknowledgment would be complete without a word of thanks to all who helped in the gathering and research of the material in this book. Many fellow teachers, parents and friends shared their collected and recollected rhythms with me. In looking for sources which might carry fragments or published versions of the work which would eventually be included in this compilation, my search was greatly aided by the ever-helpful assistance and concern of the librarians I had occasion to consult: Pittsburgh and Dormont, Pennsylvania; Frederick, Maryland; Richmond and Bon Air, Virginia; Philadelphia and Elkins Park, Pennsylvania.

A final acknowledgment and special thank you go to the young people with whom I used these rhythms, from Kindergarten and primary classes to my own five children. (And to my husband, whose support never faltered.) Their laughter and their love are the basic rhythms and wellsprings of life.

Gloria T. Delamar

Foreword

A WORD TO THE YOUNG PEOPLE WHO MIGHT USE THIS BOOK: The rhythms in this book were put together for you to enjoy. These are the fingerplays, join-in rhythms, chants for jump-rope and ball-bounce, tongue-twisters, rhymes and tales which young people everywhere seem to like. Most can be enjoyed alone or in groups. They were gathered for you with love.

TO TEACHERS, LIBRARIANS, PARENTS AND OTHERS:

This is a reference book of material for children that stands alone in educational value at the same time that it supplements the general curriculum. The extra-curricular Three R's — Rhythm, Rhyme, and Repetition — are used as important adjuncts to the traditional Three R's — Reading, 'Riting, and 'Rithmetic. The material in this book offers extra-curricular aid through exercises, games, and verses; with alphabets, with numbers, and with other informational subjects; as well as with rhythms that encourage and enhance both small-muscle and large-muscle development and control.

Each chapter actually constitutes a comprehensive collection. Chapter introductions state the specific value and use of the particular rhythms. These are the "fun" reinforcements of the total learning experience. Children do find them entertaining and enjoyable. Their use also lies beyond the classroom — at home and at play. They illustrate perfectly how something need not be dull or seem like "work" to be of value as an educational activity.

Included here are all the old traditional favorites (and some new "talking rhythms" written to meet specific needs). Up to now, those who wanted to use such rhythms and rhymes have had to search them out tediously from numerous sources. The intention of this book is to provide a comprehensive collection in a single volume.

Gloria T. Delamar
Melrose Park, Pennsylvania

Table of Contents

1. Fingerplays

ix

2. *Five-Finger-Plays*

3. More-Than-Finger-Plays

4. *Holiday Potpourri*

Valentine's Day

Easter

Halloween

Thanksgiving

5. *Join-In Rhythms*

6. *Counting-Out Rhymes*

7. *Jump-Rope and Bounce-Ball Chants*

8. *Tongue-Twisters*

9. *"Staircase" Tales*

10. Narrative Verses

Index 195

1. Fingerplays

Fingerplays have traditionally played an important role in education: teaching rhythm, muscle control, and language. They can also teach good character, provide information about certain subjects, even be useful as subtle disciplinary diversions! Children like them because they are fun to do. The verse acted out as a fingerplay gains in vividness. The fingerplay involves the use of fingers, hands and arms to help "tell" the verse. This truly is "talking with your hands," for the story is illustrated by hand positions and movements.

Pat-a-Cake

Pat-a-cake, pat-a-cake, baker's man,
Make me a cake as fast as you can;
Prick it, and pat it, and mark it with a B,
And put it in the oven for Baby and me.
— *Old English rhyme.*

Lines 1 & 2: clap hands. *Line 3*: hold out left hand, palm down; with right hand prick it, pat it, and mark it. *Line 4*: extend hands forward as though putting it in oven, then point away from self to indicate Baby, and then toward self. Very young children like to clap their hands throughout.

Rockabye Baby

Rockabye, Baby, in the tree top,
When the wind blows, the cradle will rock.
When the bough breaks, the cradle will fall,
And down will come Baby, cradle and all.
— *Old American rhyme.*

Line 1: make cradle of hands, interlocking fingers, and hold arms up a bit. *Line 2*: rock the "cradle." *Line 3*: make cradle rock and fall down. *Line 4*: continue to rock cradle, low this time.

1

Here's the Church

Here's the church
And here's the steeple,
Open the door
And here are the people.

Close the door
While the people pray,
Open the door
And they all walk away.

— Old American rhyme.

VERSE 1 — *Line 1*: interlock hands with fingers pointing in toward palms, backs of fingers will form flat roof. *Line 2*: raise both index fingers, tips touching to form steeple. *Line 3*: thumbs represent church door, open them out. *Line 4*: show fingers inside for people. VERSE 2 — *Lines 1 & 2*: close thumbs back up. *Line 3*: open thumbs again. *Line 4*: fingers walk to lap.

Brownie

This is Brownie's dog house and
This is Brownie's bed
This is the pan that holds his milk
And other good things he's fed.
This is the collar that goes round his neck
With Brownie in letters new,
And this is his ball, just give it a toss
And he'll bring it right back to you.

— Author unknown.

Line 1: make teepee shape with hands, fingertips touching. *Line 2*: hold out right hand flat. *Lines 3 & 4*: cup hands together like a pan. *Lines 5 & 6*: make circle, thumbs touching and index fingers touching. *Line 7*: same shape as collar, but throw it out. *Line 8*: reach hands down to receive ball.

The Noble Duke of York

The noble Duke of York,
Had ten thousand men.
He marched them up-up-up the hill,

And marched them down again.
When they're up, they're up
And when they're down they're down,
But when they're only halfway up,
They're neither up nor down.
—Author unknown.

Lines 1 & 2: spread out all ten fingers to show them. *Line 3*: "walk" fingers up into the air. *Line 4*: walk fingers back down. *Line 5*: walk fingers back up. *Line 6*: walk fingers back down. *Lines 7 & 8*: put hands at halfway point and spread out fingers.

The Family's Things

Here are mother's knives and forks,
Here is father's table,
Here is sister's looking glass,
And here is baby's cradle.
—Author unknown.

Line 1: with backs of hands touching, slightly interlock fingers, but let them stand straight up to indicate knives and forks. *Line 2*: keeping fingers interlocked, turn hands over so that the backs of the hands are uppermost, with the fingertips inside the palms and the knuckles forming a table. *Line 3*: raise the index fingers from the table so that they form a triangle with the tips touching to indicate a looking glass. *Line 4*: now raise the little fingers in the same positions as the index fingers and rock the hands to indicate a cradle rocking.

Big Eyes

See my big and scary eyes,
Look out now, a big surprise —
BOO!
—Author unknown.

Line 1: point to eyes, opening them wide. *Line 2*: cover face with both hands. *Line 3*: quickly remove hands and shout "boo."

Shake Them, Shake Them

Shake them, shake them,
Give a little clap,

Shake them, shake them,
Put them in your lap,
Shake them, shake them,
Tie a little shoe,
Shake them, shake them
And play peek-a-boo!

— *Author unknown*.

Lines 1, 3, 5 & 7: shake both hands. *Line 2*: clap. *Line 4*: put hands in lap. *Line 6*: bend over and pretend to tie shoe. *Line 8*: hide face behind hands and then open them at words "peek-a-boo!"

Pancake

Mix a pancake,
Stir a pancake,
Pop it in the pan;
Fry the pancake,
Toss the pancake,
Catch it if you can.

— Christina G. Rosetti,
Sing-Song, 1871.

Mix, stir, etc., following action of verse as spoken.

Let Us Chase the Squirrel

Let us chase the squirrel,
Up the hickory, down the hickory,
Let us chase the squirrel,
Up the hickory tree.
If you want to catch me,
Up the hickory, down the hickory,
If you want to catch me,
Learn to climb a tree.

— *Annie L. Preston*.*

Line 1: left arm hanging down represents the hickory. Right hand moves toward bottom of tree with fingers in a running motion. *Line 2*: right hand runs up hickory, then back down. *Line 3*: right hand moves back and forth near hickory. *Line 4*: right hand runs up tree. *Line 5*: hand

---

*From Holiday Songs and Every Day Songs and Games, *by Emilie Poulsson, Milton Bradley Co., 1906.

moves back and forth. *Line 6*: hand runs up, then back down. *Line 7*: hand moves back and forth. *Line 8*: climb slowly up the tree instead of running.

Birdies Flying

Birdies flying to and fro,
Flying high and flying low,
Perching in the leafy tree,
Or on earth when worms they see,
Birdies flying east and west,
Then returning to their nest.

—*Gloria T. Delamar*.

Line 1: flutter hands to indicate birds flying. *Line 2*: flutter high, then low. *Line 3*: raise both arms straight up to represent tree. *Line 4*: bend and let one finger wiggle on ground to represent worm. *Line 5*: move arms from side to side, with fingers fluttering. *Line 6*: make cup of hands to represent nest.

A-hunting

A-hunting we will go,
A-hunting we will go.
We'll catch a fox
And put him in a box,
And then we'll let him go.

—*Author unknown*.

Lines 1 & 2: place right hand on forehead shading eyes, as though searching. *Lines 3 & 4*: cross both hands and arms over chest. *Line 5*: spread both arms wide as though releasing fox.

Fireflies

Winking, blinking, winking, blinking,
See that little light.
Now it's here,
Now it's there,
Now it's out of sight.
Winking, blinking, winking, blinking,
Fireflies at night.

—*Author unknown*.

Lines 1 & 2: open and shut hand to indicate winking and blinking. *Line 3*: continue to blink hand near body. *Line 4*: continue to blink hand with arm extended. *Line 5*: hide hand behind back. *Lines 6 & 7*: continue to blink hand in front of you.

Eensy Weensy Spider

Eensy weensy spider went up the water spout.
Down came the rain and washed the spider out.
Out came the sun and dried up all the rain.
So eensy weensy spider went up the spout again.
— *Author unknown.*

Line 1: run up one arm with fingers of other hand. *Line 2*: flutter fingers of both hands in downward stroke. *Line 3*: join hands over head to make large circle. *Line 4*: run up arm again.

Grandma

Here are Grandma's spectacles,
And here is Grandma's cap,
And this is the way she folds her hands
And puts them in her lap.
— *Author unknown.*

Line 1: make a circle with each hand (index finger to thumb) and place one circle in front of each eye for spectacles. *Line 2*: put hands on head, fingers touching to form a peak, to make cap. *Lines 3 & 4*: fold hands and put them in lap.

Little Bunny

Here's a little bunny
On a shelf in the shop,
Wind him up slowly,
And away he'll hop.
— *Author unknown.*

Line 1: raise the index and middle fingers to represent rabbit's ears. *Line 2*: sit the rabbit hand on the back of the other hand. *Line 3*: make rotating motions beside rabbit hand as though winding him up. *Line 4*: make rabbit hand hop away.

In and Out

In and out, in and out,
Now I roll my hands about,
First up high and then down low,
This is the way my fingers go.
— Author unknown.

Line 1: at word "in" put hands close to body, and at word "out" stretch them out in front of you. *Line 2*: circle hands around each other. *Line 3*: put hands up high, then put them low. *Line 4*: palms up, show hands.

The Meadow

This is the meadow where all the long day,
Ten little frolicsome lambs are at play.
These are the measure the good farmer brings,
Salt in, or cornmeal, and other good things.

This is the lambkins' own big water-trough,
Drink, little lambkins, and then scamper off!
This is the rock where in winter they feed;
Hay makes a very good dinner indeed.

These are the big shears to shear the old sheep;
Dear little lambkins their soft wool may keep.
Here, with its big double doors shut so tight,
This is the barn where they all sleep at night.
— Emilie Poulsson.*

VERSE 1 — *Lines 1 & 2*: put arms down and slightly forward, hands clasped. *Lines 3 & 4*: cup both hands. VERSE 2 — *Lines 1 & 2*: cup hands together to make a trough. *Lines 3 & 4*: clasp hands together in double fist, thumbs inside fists. VERSE 3 — *Lines 1 & 2*: extend index and middle fingers in snipping movements of shears. *Lines 3 & 4*: clasp hands together in double fist, with thumbs outside for barn doors.

A Cup of Tea

Here's a cup, and here's a cup,
And here's a pot of tea.

---

*Fingerplays for Nursery & Kindergarten, *Lothrop, Lee, & Shepard, Boston, 1893.*

Pour one cup, pour another cup,
Come and drink with me.
— Author unknown.

Line 1: each hand cupped represents a cup. *Line 2*: put both hands together in ball shape. *Line 3*: pretend to pour into each cup. *Line 4*: put one cup to mouth to drink.

Creeping

Creeping, creeping
To my head.
Take them down again,
And put them all to bed.
— Author unknown.

Lines 1 & 2: very slowly let the hands creep up to the head. *Lines 3 & 4*: take them down and quickly fold hands.

The Mice

Five little mice on the pantry floor,
Seeking for bread crumbs or something more.
Five little mice on the shelf up high,
Feasting so daintily on a pie.

But the big round eyes of the wise old cat
See what five little mice are at.
Quickly she jumps! — but the mice run away,
And hide in their snug little holes all day.

"Feasting in pantries may be very nice;
But home is the best!" say the five little mice.
— Emilie Poulsson. *

VERSE 1 — *Lines 1 & 2*: hold up right hand to represent mice. *Lines 3 & 4*: put up left hand and rest mice fingers on top of it (left hand is shelf). VERSE 2 — *Lines 1 & 2*: indicate eyes of cat by making a small circle with each hand, index finger to middle finger. *Lines 3 & 4*: left hand comes from side, quickly pouncing as the right hand quickly runs away to its side. VERSE 3 — *Lines 1 & 2*: clasp hands for home.

*Fingerplays for Nursery & Kindergarten, *Lothrop, Lee, & Shepard, Boston, 1893.*

A Little Boy Went Walking

A little boy went walking
One lovely summer day,
He saw a little rabbit
That quickly ran away.
He saw the shining river
Go winding in and out,
And little fishes in it
Were playing all about.

And slowly, slowly turning
The great wheel of the mill
And then the high church steeple
The little church so still.
The bridge across the water
And as he stopped to rest
He saw among the bushes
A little sparrow's nest.

And as he watched the birdies
Above the tree-tops fly
He saw the clouds all sailing
Across the summer sky.
He saw the bugs all crawling
The flowers that summer brings
He said, "I'll go tell mother
I have seen so many things."
— *Emilie Poulsson.**

VERSE 1 — *Lines 1 & 2*: walk with right index and middle fingers. *Lines 3 & 4*: raise left index and middle fingers for rabbit ears. *Lines 5 & 6*: move both hands in wavy lines beside each other to indicate the river. *Lines 7 & 8*: wiggle both index fingers to and fro. VERSE 2 — *Lines 1 & 2*: circle hands around each other. *Lines 3 & 4*: make steeple of hands, palms apart and fingertips touching. *Lines 5 & 6*: point thumbs down and interlock straight fingers. *Lines 7 & 8*: cup hands to form a nest. VERSE 3 — *Lines 1 & 2*: flutter fingers with arms up. *Lines 3 & 4*: one hand and arm moving slowly overhead. *Line 5*: crawl fingers of both hands. *Line 6*: fingers turned up like petals. *Lines 7 & 8*: point to eyes, then fold hands.

*Fingerplays for Nursery & Kindergarten, *Lothrop, Lee, & Shepard, Boston, 1893.*

The Pigs

Piggie Wig and Piggie Wee,
Hungry pigs as pigs could be,
For their dinner had to wait
Down behind the barnyard gate.

Piggie Wig and Piggie Wee
Climbed the barnyard gate to see,
Peeping through the gate so high,
But no dinner could they spy.

Piggie Wig and Piggie Wee
Got down sad as pigs could be;
But the gate soon opened wide
As they scampered forth outside.

Piggie Wig and Piggie Wee
What was their delight to see
Dinner ready not far off —
Such a full and tempting trough!

Piggie Wig and Piggie Wee,
Greedy pigs as pigs could be,
For their dinner ran pellmell;
In the trough both pigs fell.

       — *Emilie Poulsson.*[*]

VERSE 1 — *Lines 1, 2 & 3*: put fingertips of right hand against fingertips of left hand, with palms toward body. Raise thumbs to represent pigs. *Line 4*: put thumbs down behind hands (gate). VERSE 2 — *Line 3*: poke thumbs out of gate between index and middle fingers as pigs peek through gate. VERSE 3 — *Lines 1 & 2*: put thumbs back behind gate again. *Line 3*: open hands as gate opens. *Line 4*: wriggle thumbs forward as pigs scamper forth. VERSE 4 — *Lines 1 & 2*: with hand in fist, raise thumbs to show pig. *Lines 3 & 4*: make cup of hands to represent trough. VERSE 5 — *Lines 1, 2 & 3*: wriggle thumbs over cupped hands. *Line 4*: pop thumbs into cup of hand as pigs fall into trough.

All for Baby

Here's a ball for Baby,
Big and soft and round.

---

[*]Fingerplays for Nursery & Kindergarten, *Lothrop, Lee, & Shepard, Boston, 1893.*

Here's the Baby's hammer,
Oh, how he can pound.

Here is Baby's music
Clapping, clapping so.
Here are Baby's soldiers,
Standing in a row.

Here's the Baby's trumpet,
Toot-too-toot, toot-too.
Here's the way the Baby,
Plays a peek-a-boo.

Here's a big umbrella,
Keeps the Baby dry.
Here's the Baby's cradle,
Rock-a-Baby-bye.

—*Emilie Poulsson.* *

VERSE 1 — *Lines 1 & 2*: show a ball with both hands, fingertips touching. *Lines 3 & 4*: pound fists one on top of the other. VERSE 2 — *Lines 1 & 2*: clap. *Lines 3 & 4*: hold all ten fingers up. VERSE 3 — *Lines 1 & 2*: hold hands out as though holding a trumpet. *Lines 3 & 4*: hide head behind hands and remove at "peek-a-boo." VERSE 4 — *Lines 1 & 2*: put left index finger under right palm, forming a handle and umbrella top. *Lines 3 & 4*: interlock fingers, palms up, and rock hands.

My Garden Bed

In my little garden bed
Raked so nicely over,
First the tiny seeds I sow,
Then with soft earth cover.

Shining down, the great round sun
Smiles upon it often;
Little raindrops, pattering down,
Help the seeds to soften.

Then the little plant awakes!
Down the roots go creeping.
Up it lifts its little head
Through the brown mould peeping.

*Fingerplays for Nursery and Kindergarten, *Lothrop, Lee, & Shepard, Boston, 1893.*

High and higher still it grows
Through the summer hours,
Till some happy day the buds
Open into flowers.

— Emilie Poulsson. *

VERSE 1 — *Line 1*: interlock fingers, with palms up. *Line 2*: scratch with fingers of one hand for rake. *Line 3*: gently shake hand as though sowing seeds. *Line 4*: use both hands in patting motion as though patting the earth over the seeds. VERSE 2 — *Lines 1 & 2*: raise arms over head with hands touching to make big circle representing sun. *Lines 3 & 4*: with arms still up, start descending slowly with fingertips fluttering as raindrops patter down. VERSE 3 — *Lines 1 & 2*: hold hand down and stiffly point fingers down to represent roots. *Lines 3 & 4*: make fist and start to raise thumb from it as the plant starts growing. VERSE 4 — *Lines 1 & 2*: elevating the arm, continue to raise thumb from fist. *Lines 3 & 4*: open hand and spread fingers to represent flower in bloom.

Three Balls

A little ball,
A bigger ball,
A great big ball you see.
Let's count the balls
That we have made;
One,
Two,
Three.

— Author unknown.

Line 1: make a small circle, joining right index finger to right thumb. *Line 2*: using both hands, make circle joining index fingers together and thumbs together. *Line 3*: spread arms to make large circle with hands touching. *Lines 4 & 5*: simply hold hands still. *Line 6*: repeat actions for line 1. *Line 7*: repeat actions for line 2. *Line 8*: repeat actions for line 3.

Garden Bed

Come see my small garden, how sweetly they grow,
My five pretty blossoms, all here in a row.
The rose and the pansy, the lily so tall,
The phlox and forget-me-not, smallest of all.

*Fingerplays for Nursery and Kindergarten, Lothrop, Lee, & Shepard, Boston, 1893.

My blossoms are thirsty, so now I will bring
Cool water and sprinkle each dear little thing.
The dew helps me bathe them, the sun bids them grow,
And their beauty rewards all the care I bestow.
— *Kate Whiting Patch.* *

VERSE 1 — *Lines 1 & 2*: hold up five fingers of right hand. *Lines 3 & 4*: start with thumb for rose, touch each finger in succession to the little finger for forget-me-not. VERSE 2 — *Lines 1 & 2*: pretend to sprinkle right hand with left hand. *Line 3*: form sun by making large circle with both hands. *Line 4*: return hands to lap.

The Caterpillar's Life

A caterpillar crawled, all furry and brown,
Until it was time to lay himself down.
He spun a cocoon of silvery gray,
And slept all winter until a spring day.
The cocoon awoke when the sun came out,
Inside a creature stirred about.
Suddenly there appeared a head,
Looking down at the tulip bed;
And what should emerge and gaily fly,
But a beautiful, golden butterfly.
— *Gloria T. Delamar.*

Lines 1 & 2: make fist, but extend thumb and wiggle it forward as though crawling. *Lines 3 & 4*: hold fist still, rotate thumb in circle and then fold thumb. *Lines 5 & 6*: stir hand back and forth. *Lines 7 & 8*: pop thumb out as head looks around. *Lines 9 & 10*: place both thumbs back to back for butterfly's body and flap palms for wings.

A Little Plant

In the heart of a seed,
Buried down so deep,
A little plant
Lay fast asleep.

"Awake," said the sun,
"Come up through the earth,"

*From Timely Games & Songs for the Kindergarten, by Clare Sawyer Reed, J.L. Hammet Co., 1900.

"Awake," said the rain,
"We are giving you birth."

The little plant heard
With a happy sigh,
And pointed its petals
Up to the sky.

— *Author unknown.*

VERSE 1: make fist to represent seed. VERSE 2 — *Lines 1 & 2*: make large circle with hands to indicate sun. *Lines 3 & 4*: flutter fingertips down to indicate falling rain. VERSE 3: open hand and turn up fingers for petals and raise wrist as plant grows.

Leaves, Flowers, and Fruits

Oh! Here are the little leaves that grow
Upon the great tall trees,
And dance so merrily all day
With every passing breeze.

Oh! Here are the pretty buds of green,
And closely shut are they;
But on the trees they grow and grow,
Then open wide some day.

Oh! Here are the sweet and dainty flowers
To which the green buds grow,
The fragrant blossoms, rosy pink
Or fair and white as snow.

Oh! Here are the juicy fruits at last,
All ripe upon the trees;
They're ready for the children now,
Who'll have a taste of these?

— *Alice May Douglas.* *

VERSE 1: move fingers rapidly to represent fluttering leaves. VERSE 2: bring five fingers together, the tips touching, each hand representing a bud. VERSE 3: let buds gradually open to flowers, spreading out fingers for petals. VERSE 4: double up fists for fruits.

*From Nursery Rhyme Book, *by Andrew Lang, Frederick Warne Co., 1897.*

The Seed and the Rain

Take the little seed so hard and round
Make a little hole down in the ground,
Put the seed into it, cover it with care,
Will it ever leave the earth so brown?
Wait and watch it closely when the rain comes down.

Soon a small green stalk grows high in the air,
And a little bud is showing there.
And the pleasant sunshine quickly brings to view,
White and yellow daisies, fresh and new.
Though the dusty road may make them brown,
They will sparkle brightly when the rain comes down.
—Author unknown.

VERSE 1 — *Line 1*: show right fist. *Line 2*: burrow fist down. *Lines 3, 4, &
5*: cover right fist with left hand. *Line 6*: raise left arm and flutter fingers
down to right fist. VERSE 2 — *Line 1*: raise right wrist. *Line 2*: open fist and
form bud with fingers up and touching each other. *Line 3*: raise left arm
and hover hand above. *Lines 4 & 5*: open right hand to indicate petals
opening. *Line 6*: flutter left hand down to right hand.

Right Hand, Left Hand

Right hand, left hand, put them on my head.
Right hand, left hand, put them all to bed.
Right hand, left hand, put them on my chest.
Right hand, left hand, put them all to rest.
—Author unknown.

Show right and left hands where indicated, put on head and chest and on
lap for bed and rest.

Rain

It drizzles, it rains,
It pours, it hails.
It lightnings, it thunders,
All the children run home.
—Author unknown.

To be done on a table or on the floor. *Line 1*: tap on table with fingers in pattering sound. *Line 2*: rap knuckles on table. *Line 3*: one hand waves through the air and then both fists pound on the table. *Line 4*: move fingers in running motion until they are in lap.

Flowers Grow

This is the way the flowers sleep,
Through the winter long.
This is the way the flowers grow,
When they hear the robin's song.
—Author unknown.

Lines 1 & 2: make fists of both hands. *Line 3*: open hands. *Line 4*: raise arms until they represent a full grown flower.

Ladybug

Ladybug, ladybug, fly away home,
Your house is on fire,
And your children will burn.
All but one, her name is Ann,
And she crept under the frying pan.
—Author unknown.

Line 1: flutter both hands in flying motion. *Lines 2 & 3*: shoot arms up and down in air several times. *Line 4*: raise one hand to represent Ann. *Line 5*: have Ann crawl under palm of other hand which is the frying pan.

Raindrops

Ten little raindrops dancing on the walk,
Pitter patter, pitter patter, that's the way they talk.
Out comes the yellow sun shining in the sky,
And away all the raindrops fly, fly, fly.
—Author unknown.

Lines 1 & 2: tap fingers on floor. *Line 3*: make large circle with fingers for sun. *Line 4*: fingers hurry away to hide behind back.

The Snow

This is the way the snow comes down,
Upon a winter day,

But soon the golden sun comes out,
And melts it all away.
>   —*Author unknown*.

Lines 1 & 2: flutter fingers down from arms raised position until arms are lowered. *Lines 3 & 4*: make large circle with fingers for sun.

Snowdrops

Here is brown bulb, small and round,
Hiding safely below the ground,
Two little leaves begin to grow,
Peeping out above the snow.
Last comes snowdrop, small and white,
Nodding gaily to greet the light.
>   —*Author unknown*.

Line 1: make fist of right hand. *Line 2*: cover right fist with left hand. *Lines 3 & 4*: extend index and middle fingers. *Lines 5 & 6*: open right hand to form flower and raise, letting left hand slide down right wrist.

Making a Snowman

Roll a snowball round and round,
Round and round upon the ground.
Make one, make two, here's what you do,
You can build a snowman too.
As the sun shines down some day,
Poor snowman, he will melt away.
>   —*Gloria T. Delamar*.

Lines 1 & 2: roll hands around each other. *Line 3*: make two fists, then put one on top of the other. *Lines 4 & 5*: hold fists in snowman position. *Line 6*: open hands flat out on top of each other.

Birds on a Stone

Two little birds, sat on a stone,
One flew away and that left one.
The other flew after and then there were none.
Of those two birds, one back again flew,
The other flew after, and then there were two.
Said the one to the other, "How do you do."
"Very well," said the other, "and how are you?"
>   —*Author unknown*.

Line 1: put both hands on knees. *Line 2*: right hand goes behind back.
Line 3: left hand goes behind back. *Line 4*: right hand returns to knee.
Line 5: left hand returns to knee. *Line 6*: bob right hand. *Line 7*: bob left
hand.

Pease Porridge

Pease porridge hot,
Pease porridge cold,
Pease porridge in a pot,
Nine days old.
Some like it hot,
Some like it cold,
Some like it in a pot,
Nine days old.

— Old English rhyme.

Simple version: *Lines 1, 3, 5, 7*: clap hands. *Lines 2, 4, 6, 8*: tap hands on
knees. For a more involved version, the action changes with each word,
using five basic motions. 1. clap thighs with both hands. 2. clap. 3. extend
right hand in front (if done with a partner, partners clap right hands
together). 4. extend left hand in front (if done with a partner, partners
clap left hands together). 5. extend both hands in front (partners would
then clap left hand to partner's right and vice versa). Perform thus:

Pease porridge hot, 1, 2, 3
Pease porridge cold, 1, 2, 4
Pease porridge in a pot, 1, 2, 3, 2
Nine days old. 4, 2, 5
Some like it hot, 1, 2, 3
Some like it cold, 1, 2, 4
Some like it in a pot, 1, 2, 3, 2
Nine days old. 4, 2, 5

Big Indians

There were five great big Indians;
    (Refrain)
    They stood so straight and tall,
    They tried to fit in a little canoe,
    And one of them did fall.
There were four great big Indians;
    (Refrain)
There were three great big Indians;

(Refrain)
There were two great big Indians;
(Refrain)
There was one great big Indian;
He stood so straight and tall,
And he did fit in the little canoe,
And he paddled it right home.
—Author unknown.

One hand represents Indians and the other the canoe. Try to fit number of fingers into canoe as mentioned in the verse.

Indians and Trees

This is a forest of long long ago—
There are the trees standing all in a row.
Look very closely, what do you see?
Indians peering out—one, two, three.
Now they are hiding. The forest is still.
Now they are hurrying over the hill.
Ever so quietly, now they are nearing
The teepees that stand at the edge of the clearing.
—Author unknown.

Lines 1, 2, & 3: hold up left hand. *Line 4:* poke three fingers of right hand through fingers of left hand. *Line 5:* hide right fingers again. *Lines 6 & 7:* make fist (hill) of left hand and walk right hand over it. *Line 8:* make teepee with both hands, palms apart and fingertips up and touching.

Ten Little Indians

Ten little Indians standing in a line,
Ten little Indians strong, straight, and fine.
Ten little Indians' tomahawks wave high,
Ten little Indians yell a war cry. Wahoo!
Ten little Indians ride far out of sight,
Ten little Indians come home safe at night.
Ten little Indians to their wigwams creep,
Ten little Indians now are fast asleep.
—Author unknown.

Lines 1 & 2: all fingers stand straight. *Line 3:* pretend to wave tomahawk high over head with one hand. *Line 4:* move hand back and forth in front of mouth. *Line 5:* put hands behind back. *Line 6:* fingers ride back to front of body. *Line 7*: put fingers straight through each other with tips up. (This will look like a row of wigwams.) *Line 8*: put head on back of hands in prayer position.

I Can Make My Fingers Go

I have ten little fingers
And they all belong to me.
I can make them do things;
Would you like to see?

I can shut them up tight,
Or open them wide.
I can put them together,
Or make them all hide.

I can make them jump high,
I can make them jump low.
I can fold them up quietly
And hold them just so.
> — *Author unknown.*

VERSE 1: hold up all ten fingers. VERSE 2 — *Line 1*: close both hands. *Line 2*: open both hands. *Line 3*: fold hands together. *Line 4*: hide both hands behind back. VERSE 3 — *Line 1*: raise hands high. *Line 2*: put hands low. *Lines 3 & 4*: fold hands in lap.

Two Hands Have I

Two hands have I to hold in sight,
One is the left, the other the right,
Five busy fingers I have on each,
Just made to hold a plum or a peach.
Made to pound, and made to clap,
And made to fold onto my lap.
> — *Author unknown.*

Line 1: hold up both hands. *Line 2*: indicate left and right hands by shaking hand when saying identifying word. *Line 3*: hold up both hands. *Line 4*: make fist of each hand. *Line 5*: pound fists, then clap. *Line 6*: fold hands in lap.

In the Sky

In the sky in daytime light,
We can see the sunshine bright.
We can see the clouds puffed white,
Moving slowly in their flight.

In the sky in black midnight,
We can see the moon's clear light,
We can see the stars in sight,
Twinkling high with all their might.
— *Gloria T. Delamar*.

VERSE 1 — *Line 1*: stretch arms up. *Line 2*: keep arms up and make a circle
with fingers. *Lines 3 & 4*: wave hands slowly. VERSE 2 — *Line 1*: stretch
arms up. *Line 2*: keep arms up and make a circle with fingers. *Lines 3 &
4*: wiggle fingers to indicate twinkling stars.

The Moon

Pointing left, the waxing moon;
Increasing, it is growing.
Pointing right, the waning moon;
Decreasing, it is going.
The time that shines between the two,
Is full moon in the midnight blue.
    Waxing moon —
    Waning moon —
    Full moon!
— *Gloria T. Delamar*.

Lines 1 & 2: make crescent (semi-circle) with right index finger and
thumb, which will result in the points of the crescent pointing left to the
eyes of the performer. *Lines 3 & 4*: make crescent with left index finger
and thumb. *Lines 5 & 6*: join the crescents to make a full moon circle.
Line 7: raise right arm and make a large crescent. *Line 8*: raise left arm
and make a large crescent. *Line 9*: join hands at top to make a large full
moon circle.

The Earth

The earth is a great big ball,
It isn't flat at all.

It spins around just like a top,
I'm sure that it will never stop.
                              — *Author unknown.*

Line 1: shape ball with hands, thumbs touching and fingertips touching. *Line 2:* put palms together, back of one hand facing up and the other down. *Line 3:* spin index fingers around each other. *Line 4:* fold hands together.

The Seasons

In spring, the gently falling rain,
Makes the earth all green again.
In summer, sun shines on the ground,
And we see flowers all around.
In autumn, winds blow round us all,
To make the leaves turn brown and fall.
In winter, snow drifts white and deep,
To make a blanket for earth's sleep.
                              — *Gloria T. Delamar.*

Line 1: flutter fingers downward. *Line 2:* make a ball of hands to represent earth. *Line 3:* make ball overhead to represent sun. *Line 4:* hold hands up with fingertips forming petals. *Line 5:* pass hands back and forth in front of chest. *Line 6:* close hand at fingertips, raise arms and move hands down in a wavy motion. *Line 7:* with open hands, bring arms down in wavy motion. *Line 8:* cover one fist with palm of other hand.

Five Little Farmers

Five little farmers
Woke up with the sun,
For it was early morning
And chores must be done.

The first little farmer
Went to milk the cow.
The second little farmer
Thought he'd better plow.

The third little farmer
Fed the hungry hens.
The fourth little farmer
Mended broken pens.

The fifth little farmer
Took his vegetables to town,
Baskets filled with cabbages
And sweet potatoes, brown.

When the work was finished
And the western sky was red,
Five little farmers,
Tumbled into bed.

—Author unknown.

VERSE 1 *— Lines 1 & 2*: show a fist with one hand. *Lines 3 & 4*: open hand, put all fingers upright. VERSE 2 *— Lines 1 & 2*: fingers of both hands closed under thumbs, move up and down as if milking. *Lines 3 & 4*: fingers of both hands closed under thumbs as if holding plow, move hands to right and left. VERSE 3 *— Lines 1 & 2*: with right fingers toss out feed held in left hand. *Lines 3 & 4*: close fingers of right hand over thumb as if holding hammer, move arm up and down. VERSE 4 *— All lines*: use both hands to hold imaginary wheel, move it as though driving. VERSE 5 *— All lines*: close fingers of one hand into a fist as in beginning.

Mr. Turkey and Mr. Duck

Mr. Turkey took a walk one day
In the very best of weather.
Along came Mr. Duck
And they both talked together.
Gobble, gobble, gobble,
Quack, quack, quack,
Good-bye, good-bye,
And they both walked back.

—Author unknown.

Lines 1 & 2: walk out right hand with fingers spread for turkey's tail. *Lines 3 & 4*: walk out left hand. *Line 5*: open and close right hand. *Line 6*: open and close left hand. *Line 7*: both hands open and close in turn. *Line 8*: walk both hands behind back.

The Funny Men

There's a funny little house,
On a funny little street,
And the funniest thing you know —
There's a funny little man

In that funny little house,
It's hard to believe, but it's so.

And right across the street,
There's another little house
And another little man,
And they play hide-and-seek
All the day.

Out of his window
The first little man peeps,
Sees no one stirring
Across the street,
And out of his door
He creeps so slow,
Looks up, looks down, looks high, looks low,
And back into his house he goes.

Then out of his window
The other little man peeps,
Sees no one stirring,
Across the street,
And out of his door
He creeps so slow,
Looks up, looks down, looks high, looks low,
And back into his house he goes.

But sometimes these men
Forget to peep,
And out of their doors
So slowly creep,
Look up, look down, look high, look low,
And back into their houses go.
                              —*Author unknown.*

Each fist indicates a house, and each thumb indicates one of the funny little men. As the verse is spoken, the thumbs perform the motions of the men coming out, looking up, down, high, low, and going back into the houses.

Whisky, Frisky

Whisky, frisky, hippity hop,
Up he goes, to the tree-top.
Whirly, twirly, round and round,

Down he scampers to the ground.
Furly, curly, what a tail.
Tall as a feather, broad as a sail.
Where's his supper? In the shell.
Snappy, cracky, out it fell.
                    —*Author unknown.*

Lines 1 & 2: raise left arm and run up to hand with fingers of right hand.
Lines 3 & 4: roll hand back down arm. *Lines 5 & 6*: spread fingers of right hand and move hand back and forth. *Line 7*: make hollow ball using both hands. *Line 8*: let hands fall apart, as a nut broken in half.

Learning

This is high, and this is low,
Only see how much I know.

This is narrow, this is wide,
Something else I know besides.

Up is where the birds fly free,
Down is where my feet should be.

This is my right hand, as you see,
This is my left hand, all agree.

Overhead I raise them high,
Clap 1, 2, 3, and let them fly.
                    —*Author unknown.*

Put hands in positions indicated by verse.

Where Is Thumbkin?

Where is *Thumbkin*?
Where is *Thumbkin*?
Here I am.
Here I am.
How are you today, sir?
Very well, I thank you.
Run away.
Run away.
                    —*Author unknown.*

(This can be sung to the tune of "Frères, Jacques.") *Lines 1 & 2*: hide both hands behind back. *Line 3*: bring out right thumb. *Line 4*: bring out left thumb. *Line 5*: wiggle right thumb. *Line 6*: wiggle left thumb. *Line 7*: hide right hand behind back again. *Line 8*: hide left hand behind back again. The entire action can be repeated for each finger of the hand, substituting for *Thumbkin*, the names *Pointer*, *Tall Man*, *Ringman*, *Pinky*, and for the whole hand *All Men*.

Ox

O
X
Is OX!

— Gloria T. Delamar.

Line 1: form large O with arms, hands touching. *Line 2*: raise both arms and cross at elbows to make X. *Line 3*: put index fingers up from head for ox horns.

Birdies on the Wire

Here are two telegraph poles,
Across them a wire is strung,
Two little birdies flying by,
Hopped on the wire and swung,
To and fro, to and fro,
Hopped on the wire and swung.

— Author unknown.

Line 1: raise both index fingers to indicate poles. *Line 2*: join middle fingertips to put a wire between the poles. *Lines 3, 4, 5, & 6*: thumbs represent birds and sit on middle fingers as birds rock to and fro.

The Zigzag Boy and Girl

I know a little zigzag boy
Who goes this way and that;
He never knows just where he put
His coat, or shoes or hat.

I know a little zigzag girl
Who flutters here and there;
She never knows just where to find
Her brush to fix her hair.

If you are not a zigzag child
You'll have no cause to say,
That you forgot, for you will know
Where things are put away.
—Author unknown.

VERSE 1—*Lines 1, 2, & 3*: put hands out in front of body and swing them back and forth in a zigzag motion. *Line 4*: point with both hands to shoulders, then to shoes, and then to top of head. VERSE 2—*Lines 1, 2, & 3*: make zigzag motions with both hands. *Line 4*: pretend to brush hair. VERSE 3—*Lines 1, 2, & 3*: make zigzag motions with both hands. *Line 4*: fold hands in lap.

Two Little Blackbirds

Two little blackbirds
Sitting on a hill.
One was named Jack
And one was named Jill.
Fly away Jack,
Fly away Jill,
Come back Jack,
Come back Jill.
Two little blackbirds
Sitting on a hill.
—Author unknown.

Lines 1 & 2: extend both index fingers. *Line 3*: bob right index finger, to indicate Jack. *Line 4*: bob left index finger, to indicate Jill. *Line 5*: put right hand behind head. *Line 6*: put left hand behind head. *Line 7*: bring back right hand. *Line 8*: bring back left hand. *Lines 9 & 10*: extend both index fingers. *Variation*: Slightly moisten two small pieces of paper and stick them to the nails of the index fingers. *Lines 1 & 2*: place the two index fingers on the edge of a table. *Line 3*: bob right index finger, to indicate Jack. *Line 4*: bob left finger, to indicate Jill. *Line 5*: swing right hand up over head and then bring back to table, this time placing the middle finger on the table edge and concealing the index finger with the little paper marking Jack. *Line 6*: repeat motions of line five with left hand. *Line 7*: swing right hand over head again, this time bringing back the index finger. *Line 8*: repeat motions of line seven with left hand. *Line 9 & 10*: rest both index fingers on the table edge.

Fish and Birds Live

The fish live in the brook,
The birds live in the tree,
But home's the very nicest place
For a little child like me.

—*Author unknown.*

Line 1: wave hands back and forth to indicate fish swimming. *Line 2*: raise hands high to indicate a tree. *Lines 3 & 4*: cross hands and arms over chest.

Jack-in-the-Box Says "Ho"

First you push him out of sight
Then drop down the cover tight
Let him go, "Ho, ho, ho,"
Jack jumps up with all his might.

—*Author unknown.*

Lines 1 & 2: push down thumb of right hand with left hand. *Lines 3 & 4*: right thumb jumps up from between fist of left hand.

Goldfish

My darling little goldfish
Hasn't any toes.
He swims around without a sound
And bumps his hungry nose.
He can't get out to play with me
Nor I get in to him.
Although I say, "Come out and play,"
He says, "Come in and swim."

—*Author unknown.*

Lines 1, 2, & 3: right hand makes wavy swimming motions. *Line 4*: right hand bumps own nose. *Line 5*: right hand swims. *Line 6*: left hand stands upright. *Line 7*: left hand motions to right hand. *Line 8*: right hand motions to left hand.

Ten Little Fishes

Ten little fishes swim to and fro,
In the water here below,
Ten little mice run along the ground,
And nobody can hear a sound.
Ten little birds fly from their nest,
Ten little birds fly home to rest.
—Author unknown.

Lines 1 & 2: move both hands in wavy swimming motions. *Lines 3 & 4*:
run all fingers on floor. *Line 5*: flutter hands as birds flying. *Line 6*: return
hands to lap.

Open, Shut Them

Open, shut them, open, shut them,
Give a little clap.
Open, shut them, open, shut them,
Fold them in your lap.
—Author unknown.

Open and shut hands, clap them, and fold them as indicated in verse.

The Senses

Little eyes see pretty things,
Little nose smells what is sweet,
Little ears hear pleasant sounds,
Mouth likes luscious things to eat.
*—I. T. Headland.**

Line 1: point to eyes. *Line 2*: point to nose. *Line 3*: point to ears. *Line 4*:
point to mouth.

A Face

Two little eyes that open and close;
Two little ears and one little nose;

*Chinese Mother Goose Rhymes, *Fleming H. Revell Co.*, 1900.

Two little cheeks and one little chin;
Two little lips with the teeth closed in!
— *Author unknown*.

Point to each part of the face as it is mentioned.

The Cobbler

The cobbler, the cobbler, makes my shoes;
He pounds them, rap, rap, rap!
He makes them small, he makes them big,
And ever he pounds, tap, tap!
— *Author unknown*.

Lines 1 & 2: pound one fist on top of the other. *Line 3*: hold hands close together for *small*, and far apart for *big*. *Line 4*: pound fists again.

Row, Row

Row, row a-fishing we'll go.
How many fishes have you, Joe?
One for my father, one for my mother,
One for my sister, one for my brother,
And one for the happy fisher boy,
Who eats his fish with yummy joy.
— *Author unknown*.

Lines 1 & 2: move arms back and forth in rowing motion. *Lines 3, 4, & 5*: unfold fingers of right hand, one by one, starting with thumb for father, and ending with little finger for boy. *Line 6*: pretend to eat with right hand and rub tummy with left hand.

The Green Leafy Tree

We went to the *meadow* and what did we see?
    A green leafy *tree*.
We went to the *meadow* and what did we see?
    A *nest* in the tree, the green leafy *tree*.
We went to the *meadow* and what did we see?
    Oh! Speckled blue *eggs* in the *nest*
    in the tree, the green leafy *tree*.
We went to the *meadow* and what did we see?
    Oh! Two baby birds from the speckled

blue eggs, the *eggs* in the *nest* in the
tree, the green leafy *tree*.
— *Author unknown*.

Show each of the italicized words with the hands as they are spoken.
Meadow: extend arms and touch fingertips. *Tree*: raise arms from sides so
that bent elbows are in line with shoulders and hands are up. *Nest*: cup
hands. *Eggs*: make an egg with each hand by touching the thumb to the
index finger. *Birds*: fly both hands overhead.

The Boy in the Barn

A little boy went into a barn,
And lay down on some hay.
An owl came out and flew about,
And the little boy ran away.
— *Author unknown*.

Lines 1 & 2: creep right hand under left hand. *Line 3*: rapidly open and
close left hand over right hand. *Line 4*: right hand runs away behind
back.

This Little Boy

This little boy is ready for bed,
Down on the pillow he puts his head,
Wraps himself in the cover tight,
And here he sleeps all the night.

When morning comes he opens his eyes,
And back with a toss the cover flies,
Up he jumps, is dressed and away,
Ready to work and play all day.
— *Author unknown*.

VERSE 1 — *Line 1*: show index finger of right hand. *Line 2*: lay right index
finger (boy) on left hand. *Lines 3 & 4*: wrap fingers of left hand around
"boy." VERSE 2 — *Lines 1 & 2*: fingers of left hand open up. *Line 3*: "boy"
jumps up, then stroke "boy" with thumb and forefinger of left hand as
though dressing him. *Line 4*: wiggle "boy" back and forth.

Now My Hands

Now my hands are on my head
Now my hands are on my shoulders
Now my fingers are like this
Now they're in my lap instead
Now my feet are on the ground
Now my lips don't make a sound.

         —Author unknown.

Lines 1, 2, & 4: do as indicated. *Line 3*: put fingertips tip to tip. *Line 5*: point to feet. *Line 6*: point to lips, whispering last line.

Jim and Jane

Here are little Jim and Jane going for a walk,
Soon the gentle rain comes down
       and spoils their little talk.
In the house the children go and to the window pane,
But every place they look they see, rain, rain, rain.
Soon again the sun shines bright,
Out come Jim and Jane.
Ready for another walk,
And all dry again.

         —Author unknown.

Line 1: walk fingers of both hands. *Line 2*: raise arms, then flutter fingers down to indicate falling rain. *Line 3*: raise arms overhead and square off hands for window. *Line 4*: flutter fingers down. *Line 5*: make circle with hands overhead for sun. *Line 6, 7, & 8*: walk fingers of both hands again.

As —— Can Be

Roll your hands, roll your hands,
    As swiftly, as swiftly, as swiftly can be.
Then roll your hands like me, like me,
    Then roll your hands like me.

Roll your hands, roll your hands,
    As slowly, as slowly, as slowly can be.
Then roll your hands like me, like me,
    Then roll your hands like me.

Clap your hands, clap your hands,
 As loudly, as loudly, as loudly can be.
Then clap your hands like me, like me,
 Then clap your hands like me.

Clap your hands, clap your hands,
 As softly, as softly, as softly can be.
Then fold your hands like me, like me,
 Then fold your hands like me.
        — *Author unknown.*

Perform with hands as words indicate.

Old Ned

Old Ned has two ears that go flop, flop, flop,
And two eyes that go blink, blink, blink,
And a mouthful of teeth that click clack when he eats,
And a tail that goes swish, swish, swish.
Old Ned has four feet that go clop, clop, clop,
And four hooves that go click, click, clack,
So he gallops, and walks, and trots, and runs,
While I sit high up on his back.
        — *Author unknown.*

Line 1: pat both ears to indicate flapping. *Line 2*: blink eyes. *Line 3*: point to mouth. *Line 4*: swish one hand back and forth. *Line 5*: tap four fingers of one hand on back of other hand. *Line 6*: snap fingers for the clicking sound. *Lines 7 & 8*: hold hands in front of body as though holding reins, and bounce body in motion of riding horse.

Traffic Lights

"Stop" says the red light,
"Go" says the green,
"Wait" says the yellow light
Blinking in between.
That's what they say and
That's what they mean.
We all must obey them —
Even the Queen.
        — *Author unknown.*

Line 1: put up hand. *Line 2*: point finger. *Lines 3 & 4*: open and shut hand. *Line 5*: indicate "stop." *Line 6*: indicate "go." *Line 7*: open and shut hand in blinking signal. *Line 8*: put hands on top of head to indicate crown.

Two Little Puppy Dogs

Two little puppy dogs
Lying in a heap,
Soft and wooly
And fast asleep.
Along came a pussycat
Creeping near, "Meow,"
She cried right in their ear.
Two little puppy dogs
After one cat,
Did you ever play tag like that?
               —Author unknown.

Lines 1, 2, 3, & 4: put out right hand, with two fingers sticking up to represent dogs. *Lines 5, 6, & 7*: from behind back, slowly let left hand creep upon dogs. At word "Meow," open hand quickly and spread fingers to indicate cat crying out. *Lines 8, 9, & 10*: right hand chases left hand away.

Mousie Brown

Up the candlestick he ran,
Little Mousie Brown,
To go and eat the tallow,
But he couldn't get back down.
He called for his Grandma,
"Grandma, Grandma,"
But his Grandma was in town,
So he doubled up into a ball,
And rolled right down.
               — Old Chinese rhyme.

Line 1: raise right arm and let the fingers of the left hand run to the top of the right hand. *Lines 2, 4, 5, 6, & 7*: let the left hand (Mousie) sit on top of right hand (candle). *Lines 8 & 9*: make fist of left hand and bring it down the right arm in a tumbling motion.

Two Little Houses

Two little houses all closed up tight,
Open up the windows and let in the light.
Ten little finger babies tall and straight,
Ready for the taxi at half past eight.
— *Author unknown.*

Line 1: put up both hands and make fists of both. *Line 2*: open fists. *Line 3*: raise fingers straight. *Line 4*: at end, put down thumbs to have eight fingers up.

Robin's Nest

Here's a nest for Robin Redbreast.
Here's a hive for busy bee.
Here's a hole for Jack Rabbit,
And a house for me.
— *Author unknown.*

Line 1: cup hands together to form a nest. *Line 2*: put hands in position of prayer, but slightly hollow between palms. *Line 3*: make circle with index fingers touching and thumbs touching to indicate a hole in the ground. *Line 4*: join hands overhead to indicate roof overhead.

The Bunny's Hole

This is the bunny with ears so funny.
And this is his hole in the ground.
When a noise he hears he pricks up his ears,
And jumps into the ground.
— *Author unknown.*

Line 1: raise two fingers of one hand (index and middle fingers). *Line 2*: make fist of other hand with a little hole in top. *Line 3*: bend and then straighten two fingers representing bunny's ears as though he were pricking them up. *Line 4*: pop bunny's ears into the hole in the other fist.

Choo-choo

This is a choo-choo train
Puffing down the track.

Now it's going forward,
Now it's going back.
Now the bell is ringing,
Now the whistle blows,
What a lot of noise it makes
Everywhere it goes.

—Author unknown.

Line 1: extend left arm, then start at shoulder and run out to the end of the arm with the right hand. *Line 2*: run right hand back to left shoulder. *Line 3*: move out to the hand again. *Line 4*: move back to the shoulder again. *Line 5*: shake right hand in movement of a bell clapper. *Line 6*: move hand up and down as though pulling chain of a train whistle. *Line 7*: run right hand (train) out to end of left arm. *Line 8*: run right hand back to left shoulder.

Right and Left Hands

This is my right hand
I'll raise it up high.
This is my left hand
I'll touch the sky.
Right hand, left hand,
Roll them around.
Left hand, right hand,
Pound, pound, pound.

—Author unknown.

Lines 1 & 2: raise right hand. *Lines 3 & 4*: raise left hand. *Line 5*: show right hand, then left hand. *Line 6*: roll hands over and over each other. *Line 7*: show left hand, then right hand. *Line 8*: pound fists together.

Five Little Soldiers

Five little soldiers
Standing in a row.
Three stood straight,
And two down so.
Along came a general,
And what do you think?
Up jumped the other two,
Quick as a wink.

—Author unknown.

Lines 1 & 2: hold up five fingers of one hand. *Line 3*: the second, third, and fourth fingers are straight. *Line 4*: the thumb and little finger are bent over. (This is easiest if the little finger is held down with the thumb.) *Lines 5 & 6*: have other hand approach the soldiers. *Lines 7 & 8*: put all five fingers up straight.

Ten Little Soldiers

Ten little soldiers
Standing in a row.
They all bow down to the captain so.
They march to the left,
They march to the right.
They all stand up straight
Ready to fight.
Along comes a man with a great big gun —
Boom — you ought to see them all run.
                                    —*Author unknown.*

Lines 1 & 2: put up both hands. *Line 3*: "bow" fingers down. *Line 4*: move hands to left in bouncing motion. *Line 5*: move hands to right. *Lines 6, 7, & 8*: put fingers up straight again. *Line 9*: clap at word "boom" and then have hands run away to hide behind back.

Bear in a Cave

Here is a cave, inside is a bear.
Now he comes out to get some fresh air.
He stays out all summer in sunshine and heat,
He hunts in the forest for berries to eat.

When snow starts to fall he hurries inside
His warm little cave and there he will hide.
When spring comes again the snow melts away,
And out comes the bear, ready to play.

He stays out all summer in sunshine and heat,
He hunts in the forest for berries to eat.
                                    —*Author unknown.*

VERSE 1 — *Line 1*: make fist of right hand. *Lines 2 & 3*: raise thumb from fist. The thumb represents the bear, and the fist is the cave. *Line 4*: spread fingers of left hand and then let bear look between fingers (forest) for berries. VERSE 2 — *Lines 1 & 2*: put thumb back into fist. *Lines 3 & 4*: raise thumb from fist. VERSE 3: spread fingers of left hand and let bear hunt for berries.

My Hands

My hands upon my head I place,
On my shoulders, on my face.
On my lips, by my side,
Then behind me they will hide.
Then I will hold them way up high,
And let my fingers quickly fly.
Hold them down in front of me,
Then I'll clap them, one, two, three.

—Author unknown.

Follow actions of verse as spoken.

Flannel The Bear Hunt

I'm going on a bear hunt.	(ALTERNATELY SLAP THIGHS)
I see a swamp	(PUT HAND AT EYEBROWS)
Can't go under it,	(SLAP THIGHS)
Can't go over it,	
Have to go through it.	
Slush, slush, slush, slush, slush.	(RUB HANDS TOGETHER)
I'm going on a bear hunt.	(SLAP THIGHS)
I see a bridge.	(HAND AT EYEBROWS)
Can't go under it,	(SLAP THIGHS)
Can't go through it,	
Have to go over it.	
Thump, thump, thump, thump, thump.	(POUND CHEST)
I'm going on a bear hunt.	(SLAP THIGHS)
I see a stream	(HAND AT EYEBROWS)
Can't go under it,	(SLAP THIGHS)
Can't go over it,	
Have to go through it.	
Splash, splash, splash, splash, splash.	(MAKE SWIMMING STROKES)

I'm going on a bear hunt.	(SLAP THIGHS)
I see a tree.	(HAND AT EYEBROWS)
Let's go see.	(SLAP THIGHS)
Up, up, up, up, up.	(FINGERS CLIMB UP)
I see a cave.	(HAND AT EYEBROWS)
Down, down, down, down, down.	(FINGERS CLIMB DOWN)
Let's go see.	(SLAP THIGHS)
I feel something.	(FEEL WITH HANDS)
I feel something furry.	
It feels like a bear.	
It looks like a bear.	
It IS a bear!	
	(PERFORM REST QUICKLY)
	(SLAP THIGHS)
Up.	(FINGERS CLIMB UP)
Down.	(FINGERS CLIMB DOWN)
	(SLAP THIGHS)
Splash, splash, splash.	(SWIMMING STROKES)
	(SLAP THIGHS)
Thump, thump, thump.	(POUND CHEST)
	(SLAP THIGHS)
Slush, slush, slush.	(RUB HANDS TOGETHER)
	(SLAP THIGHS)
WOO!	(COLLAPSE!)

—Author unknown.

Hickory, Dickory, Dock

Hickory, dickory, dock,
The mouse ran up the clock,
The clock struck one,
The mouse ran down,
Hickory, dickory, dock.

— Mother Goose rhyme.

Line 1: nod head from side to side. *Line 2*: bend left elbow, raising left hand (clock) and with right hand at left elbow, (right hand is mouse), run up to the top of the clock. *Line 3*: clap once. *Line 4*: run mouse back down clock. *Line 5*: nod head from side to side.

Jack and Jill

Jack and Jill
Went up the hill,
To fetch a pail of water.
Jack fell down
And broke his crown,
And Jill came tumbling after.

Up Jack got
And home did trot,
As fast as he could caper.
He went to bed
To mend his head,
With vinegar and brown paper.
                    — *Mother Goose rhyme.*

VERSE 1 — *Lines 1, 2, & 3:* let both hands slowly climb into the air, reaching top at the word, "water." *Lines 4 & 5:* drop one hand quickly, representing Jack falling. *Line 6:* other hand follows down with a circling, tumbling motion, representing Jill. VERSE 2 — *Lines 1, 2, & 3:* Jack moves two fingers as though running. *Lines 4, 5, & 6:* Jack hops into other hand (which is now the bed) and lies across the palm.

Little Miss Muffet

Little Miss Muffet,
Sat on a tuffet,
Eating her curds and whey.
Along came a spider
And sat down beside her,
And frightened Miss Muffet away.
                    — *Mother Goose rhyme.*

Lines 1 & 2: make fist of left hand representing Miss Muffet. Extend it forward a little. *Line 3:* pretend to eat with right hand. *Line 4:* put right hand behind back and then slowly start to bring it out again creeping like a spider. *Line 5:* spider moves up beside Miss Muffet. *Line 6:* left hand (Miss Muffet) quickly hides behind back.

Robin Redbreast

Little Robin Redbreast
Sat upon a rail,

Niddle, naddle went his head,
Wiggle, waggle went his tail.
— Mother Goose rhyme.

Lines 1 & 2: cross arms at wrists, making a fist of right hand for head, and opening out left hand for tail feathers. *Line 3*: move head up and down. *Line 4*: wiggle tail back and forth.

Humpty Dumpty

Humpty Dumpty sat on a wall,
Humpty Dumpty had a great fall.
All the King's horses and all the King's men,
Couldn't put Humpty Dumpty together again.
— Mother Goose rhyme.

Line 1: hold hands in clapping position. *Line 2*: let hands fall to lap. *Lines 3 & 4*: spread hands open in lap, palms up.

Robin Redbreast and Pussy Cat

Little Robin Redbreast sat upon a tree,
Up went Pussy Cat and down went he;
Down came the Pussy Cat, away Robin ran,
Said little Robin Redbreast, "Catch me if you can."

Little Robin Redbreast jumped upon a wall,
Pussy Cat jumped after him, and almost got a fall.
Little Robin Redbreast sang, and what did Pussy say?
Pussy Cat said, "Mew," and Robin flew away.
— Mother Goose rhyme.

VERSE 1 — *Line 1*: raise right fist. *Line 2*: raise left fist and bring down right fist. *Line 3*: bring down left fist, hide right behind back. *Line 4*: bring right half-way back out. VERSE 2 — *Line 1*: raise right fist. *Line 2*: raise left fist. *Line 3*: shake right fist. *Line 4*: shake left fist, and then fly left fist behind back.

Little Boy Blue

Little Boy Blue, come blow your horn,
The sheep's in the meadow, the cow's in the corn.
Where's the boy who takes care of the sheep?
Under the haystack, fast asleep.
— Mother Goose rhyme.

Line 1: pretend to blow horn. *Line 2*: gesture to right and then to left. *Line 3*: raise both hands questioningly. *Line 4*: rest head on folded hands.

Wee Willie Winkie

Wee Willie Winkie
Runs through the town,
Upstairs and downstairs
In his nightgown.
Rapping at the window,
Crying through the lock,
Are the children all in bed,
It's past eight o'clock.

—Mother Goose rhyme.

Lines 1 & 2: make circles with right hand. *Lines 3 & 4*: run right hand up and down left arm from elbow to fingertips. *Line 5*: knock on left hand with right. *Line 6*: put hands beside mouth as though calling. *Lines 7 & 8*: rest head on folded hands.

Jenny Wren

As little Jenny Wren
Was sitting by the shed.
She waggled with her tail,
And nodded with her head.

—Mother Goose rhyme.

Lines 1 & 2: cross arms at wrists, making fist of right hand for head, and opening out left hand for tail feathers. *Line 3*: wiggle tail. *Line 4*: nod head.

The King of France

The King of France went up the hill
With twenty thousand men;
The King of France came down the hill,
And never went up again.

—Mother Goose rhyme.

Lines 1 & 2: climb up with fingers. *Line 3*: climb back down. *Line 4*: fold hands in lap.

Sing a Song of Sixpence

Sing a song of sixpence
A pocket full of rye;
Four-and-twenty blackbirds
Baked in a pie.
When the pie was opened,
The birds began to sing;
Wasn't that a dainty dish
To set before the king?

The king was in the counting-house,
Counting all his money;
The queen was in the parlor,
Eating bread and honey.
The maid was in the garden,
Hanging out the clothes,
When along came a blackbird,
And pecked off her nose.

—Mother Goose rhyme.

VERSE 1—*Lines 1 & 2*: flutter fingers. *Lines 3 & 4*: form a circle to look like a pie. *Lines 5 & 6*: flutter fingers. *Lines 7 & 8*: form a crown on head with both hands. VERSE 2—*Lines 1 & 2*: move hands as though counting coins. *Lines 3 & 4*: make eating motions. *Lines 5 & 6*: pretend to hang up clothes. *Line 7*: right hand flies. *Line 8*: pinch nose with right hand.

Jack Horner

Little Jack Horner
Sat in a corner,
Eating a Christmas pie.
He put in his thumb,
And pulled out a plum,
And said, "What a good boy am I."

—Mother Goose rhyme.

Lines 1, 2, & 3: pretend to eat. *Line 4*: put thumb down into "pie." *Line 5*: hold up thumb. *Line 6*: pat self on head.

Jack Be Nimble

Jack be nimble,
Jack be quick
Jack jump over
The candlestick.

—Mother Goose rhyme.

Lines 1 & 2: make right index and middle fingers jump around. *Lines 3 & 4*: hold left index finger straight up and jump over it with right fingers.

Mistress Mary

Mistress Mary, quite contrary,
How does your garden grow?
With cockle shells and silver bells,
And pretty maids all in a row.

—Mother Goose rhyme.

Lines 1 & 2: place hands on hips. *Line 3*: make fists for cockle shells, then swing fingers pointed down for bells. *Line 4*: hold up ten fingers in a row.

2. Five-Finger-Plays

The five-finger-play, rather than illustrating the verse, is employed as a method of "counting" the parts of a verse. It is done by moving over the hand, touching each of the five fingers in succession, always starting with the thumb and finishing with the little finger. Sometimes, both hands are involved, with the verse having ten parts instead of five. Occasionally, the verse is one of elimination, in which case the fingers are turned down one by one until the hand is closed.

This Little Piggy

This little piggy went to market,
This little piggy stayed home.
This little piggy had roast beef,
This little piggy had none,
And this little piggy said
"Wee, wee, wee," all the way home.
— *Old American rhyme.*

John Brown Had a Little Indian

John Brown, had a little Indian,
John Brown, had a little Indian,
John Brown, had a little Indian,
One little Indian boy.

One little, two little, three little Indians,
Four little, five little, six little Indians,
Seven little, eight little, nine little Indians,
Ten little Indian boys.

Ten little, nine little, eight little Indians,
Seven little, six little, five little Indians,

45

Four little, three little, two little Indians,
One little Indian boy.
— Old American rhyme.

Five Little Froggies

This little froggie broke his toe,
This little froggie cried, "Oh, oh, oh,"
This little froggie laughed and was glad,
This little froggie cried and was sad,
But this little froggie did just as he should,
He hopped to the doctor as fast as he could.
— Author unknown.

Bunnies

"The bunnies now must go to bed,"
The furry mother bunny said.
"But I must count them first to see
If they have all come back to me.
One bunny, two bunnies, three bunnies dear,
Four bunnies, five bunnies; yes, they're all here.
They are the prettiest things alive,
My bunnies, one, two, three, four, five.
— Author unknown.

The Five Toes (or fingers)

This little cow eats grass,
This little cow eats hay,
This little cow drinks water,
This little cow runs away,
This little cow does nothing
But just lie down all day;
    WE'LL WHIP HER.
— I.T. Headland.*

Five Puppies

This little puppy said, "Let's go out to play,"
This little puppy said, "Let's run away,"

*Chinese Mother Goose Rhymes, Fleming H. Revell Co., 1900.

This little puppy said, "Let's stay out till dark,"
This little puppy said, "Let's bark, bark, bark,"
This little puppy said, "I think it would be fun,"
"To go straight home so let's run, run, run."
—Author unknown.

Squirrels

Five little squirrels sitting in a tree
The first little squirrel said, "What do I see?"
The second little squirrel said, "I see a gun."
The third little squirrel said, "Oh let's run."
The fourth little squirrel said, "Let's hide in the shade."
The fifth little squirrel said, "I'm not afraid."
When bang went the gun and away they did run.
—Author unknown.

Sugar Bunnies

Five little bunnies in a bakery shop
Shining bright with sugar on top.
Along came a boy with a penny to pay
Bought a bunny and ran away.
   (Repeat for all five fingers)
—Author unknown.

Mooly Cow

This mooly cow switched her tail all day
And this mooly cow ate the sweet meadow hay
And this mooly cow in the water did wade
And this mooly cow chewed her cud in the shade
And this mooly cow said moo the sun's gone down
It's time to take the milk to town.
—Author unknown.

This Little Bear

This little bear has a soft fur suit,
This little bear acts very cute,
This little bear is bold and cross,
This little bear rests his head on moss,

This little bear likes bacon and honey,
But he can't buy them. He has no money.
                    —*Author unknown.*

Five Snowmen

Five little snowmen
Standing in a row.
1, 2, 3, 4, 5.
Each with a hat
And a big red bow.
Five little snowmen
Dressed for show
Now they are ready,
Where will they go?
Wait 'til the sun shines.
Soon they will go,
1, 2, 3, 4, 5.
Down through the fields
With the melting snow.
                    —*Author unknown.*

Fold fingers at second count from 1 to 5.

Five Red Apples

Five red apples hanging in a tree,
The juiciest apples you ever did see.
The wind came by and gave an angry frown,
And one little apple came tumbling down.
        (Four red apples, hanging, etc.)
                    —*Author unknown.*

The Family Five

This is mother; this is father;
This is brother, strong and tall,
And beside them stands the sister
And the baby last of all.
                    —*Author unknown.*

Five Fingers

This one's old,
This one's young,
This one has no meat,
This one's gone to buy some hay,
And this one's on the street.
—*I.T. Headland.**

One Potato, Two Potato

One potato, two potato,
Three potato, four.
Five potato, six potato,
Seven potato, more.
Eight potato, nine potato,
Ten potato, then,
Start all over and do it again.
—*Old American rhyme.*

Naming the Fingers

This is little Tommy Thumb,
Round and smooth as any plum.
This is busy Peter Pointer,
Surely he's a double-jointer.
This is mighty Toby Tall,
He's the biggest one of all.
This is dainty Reuben Ring,
He's too fine for anything.
And this little wee one, maybe,
Is the pretty Finger-baby.
All the five we've counted now,
Busy fingers in a row.
Every finger knows the way
How to work and how to play;
Yet together work they best,
Each one helping all the rest.
—*Laura E. Richards.*†

*Chinese Mother Goose Rhymes, *Fleming H. Revell Co., 1900.* †*From* Songs and Music of Froebel's Mother Play, *by Susan E. Blow, D. Appleton & Co., 1895.*

The Counting Lesson

Here is the beehive. (right hand)
Where are the bees?
Hidden away where nobody sees.
Here they come creeping
Out of the hive
One! Two! Three! Four! Five!

Once I saw an ant hill (left hand)
With no ants about,
So I said, "Dear little ants,
Won't you please come out?"
Then as if the little ants
Had heard my call —
1-2-3-4-5 came out
And that was all!

— Emilie Poulsson. *

Upon Each Hand

Upon each hand
A little band
For work or play is ready.
The first to come
Is Master Thumb;
Then Pointer, strong and steady;
Then Tall Man high;
And just close by
The Feeble Man doth linger;
And last of all
So fair and small,
The baby-Little Finger.

— Emilie Poulsson. *

Ten Injuns

Ten little Injuns standing in a line,
    One went home, and then there were nine.
Nine little Injuns swinging on a gate,
    One tumbled off, and then there were eight.

*Fingerplays for Nursery and Kindergarten, Lothrop, Lee, & Shepard, Boston, 1893.

Eight little Injuns tried to get to heaven,
　　One kicked the bucket, and then there were seven.
Seven little Injuns cutting up tricks,
　　One went to bed, and then there were six.
Six little Injuns learning to dive,
　　One swam away, and then there were five.
Five little Injuns on a cellar door,
　　One jumped off, and then there were four.
Four little Injuns climbing up a tree,
　　One fell down and then there were three.
Three little Injuns out in a canoe,
　　One fell overboard, and then there were two.
Two little Injuns fooling with a gun,
　　One shot the other, and then there was one.
One little Injun living all alone,
　　He got married, and then there were none.
　　　　　　　　　—Author unknown.

Five Friends

One fat frog, sitting on a log,
　　He wanted a friend, then along came a dog.
Two little friends, playing by the sea,
　　Along came a kitten, then there were three.
Three new friends, wanted some more,
　　Along came a rabbit, then there were four.
Four friends playing, very much alive,
　　Along came a bird, then there were five.
　　　　　　　　— Gloria T. Delamar.

Ten Workers

Said the farmer, the miller, the baker,
"We'll give the dear baby his food";
Said the carpenter, glazier, and mason,
"We'll build him a house strong and good";
Said the weaver, the tailor, the cobbler,
"We'll make him warm pretty clothes";
The mechanic said, "I'll fix the auto,
When off on a journey he goes."
　　　　　　　　　—Author unknown.

The Barnyard

When the farmer's day is done,
In the barnyard, everyone,
Beast and bird politely say,
"Thank you for my food today."

The cow says, "Moo!"
The pigeon, "Coo!"
The lamb says, "Maa!"
The sheep says, "Baa!"
"Quack!" says the duck.
Says the hen, "Cluck, cluck!"
The dog, "Bow wow!"
The cat, "Meow!"
The horse says, "Neigh!"
"I love sweet hay!"
The pig near by
Grunts in his sty.

When the barn is locked up tight,
Then the farmer says, "Goodnight!"
And thanks his animals, every one,
For the work that has been done.
                              —*Author unknown.*

Five Little Pigs

The first little pig danced a merry, merry jig.
The second little pig ate candy.
The third little pig wore a blue and yellow wig.
The fourth little pig was dandy.
The fifth little pig never grew very big,
So they called him Tiny Little Andy.
                    —*Author unknown.*

This Little Squirrel

This little squirrel said, "Let's run and play."
This little squirrel said, "Let's hunt nuts today."
This little squirrel said, "Yes, nuts are good."
This little squirrel said, "They're our best food."

This little squirrel said, "Come climb this tree,
And crack these nuts, one, two, three."
—Author unknown.

This Kitty

This kitty said, "I smell a mouse,"
This kitty said, "Let's hunt through the house."
This kitty said, "Let's go creepty creep."
This kitty said, "Is the mouse asleep?"
This kitty said, "Meow, meow, I saw him go through
This hole just now."
—Author unknown.

Five Little Chickens

Said the first little chicken
With a queer little squirm,
"Oh, I wish I could find
A fat little worm!"

Said the second little chicken
With an odd little shrug,
"Oh, I wish I could find
A fat little bug!"

Said the third little chicken
With a little sigh of grief,
"Oh, I wish I could find
A green little leaf!"

Said the fourth little chicken
With a sharp little squeal,
"Oh, I wish I could find
Some nice yellow meal!"

Said the fifth little chicken
With a faint little moan,
"Oh, I wish I could find
A wee gravel stone!"

"Now see here!" said their mother,
From the green garden patch,

"If you want any breakfast,
You just come here and scratch!"
—Author unknown.

Scratch with fingers for sixth verse.

This Bunny

This bunny's ears are tall and pink,
This bunny gives a little wink.
This bunny wrinkles up his nose.
This bunny hops on his little toes.
This little one is my favorite bunny,
Because his powderpuff tail is so funny.
— Gloria T. Delamar.

Finger People

Busy little finger people,
Who will put the toys away?
I will, I will, I will, I will, I will,
All the finger people say.
—Author unknown.

Five Little Chickadees

Five little chickadees pecking at the door;
One flew away and then there were four.
Four little chickadees sitting in a tree;
One flew away and then there were three.
Three little chickadees looking at you;
One flew away and then there were two.
Two little chickadees sitting in the sun;
One flew away and then there was one.
One little chickadee left all alone;
One flew away and then there were none.
—Author unknown.

Bye, Baby Bunting

Bye, baby bunting
Father's gone a'hunting,

Mother's gone a'milking,
Sister's gone a'silking,
Brother's gone to buy a skin
To wrap the baby bunting in.
— Mother Goose rhyme.

I Caught a Hare

One, two, three, four, and five,
I caught a hare alive;
Six, seven, eight, nine, and ten,
I let him go again.
— Mother Goose rhyme.

One, Two, Buckle My Shoe

One, two, buckle my shoe;
Three, four, shut the door;
Five, six, pick up sticks;
Seven, eight, lay them straight;
Nine, ten, a big, fat hen.
— Mother Goose rhyme.

3. More-Than-Finger-Plays

While the more-than-finger-play primarily involves hand movements, body movements such as bending, jumping, or turning, are also used. This results in a slightly more energetic performance than just using finger actions!

This Old Man

This old man, he played one,
He played nick-nack on my thumb.

REFRAIN:
WITH A NICK-NACK, PADDY-WACK, GIVE A DOG A BONE,
THIS OLD MAN CAME ROLLING HOME.

This old man, he played two,
He played nick-nack on my shoe. (REFRAIN)

This old man, he played three,
He played nick-nack on my knee. (REFRAIN)

This old man, he played four,
He played nick-nack on the floor. (REFRAIN)

This old man, he played five,
He played nick-nack on my eye. (REFRAIN)

This old man, he played six,
He played nick-nack with heel kicks. (REFRAIN)

This old man, he played seven,
He played nick-nack up to heaven. (REFRAIN)

This old man, he played eight,
He played nick-nack on my plate. (REFRAIN)

This old man, he played nine,
He played nick-nack on my line. (REFRAIN)

This old man, he played ten,
He played nick-nack once again. (REFRAIN)
— *Old English folk rhyme.*

All verses: pound fists in air and then on appropriate place, i.e., knee,
floor, etc. *Refrain*: roll hands around each other.

The Chest-nut-tree

Under the *spreading*
Chest-nut-tree.
We danced happy
As we could be.
Under the *spreading*
Chest-nut-tree.

— *Author unknown.*

Perform actions as italicized words are spoken: *Under*: point hands down.
Spreading: put arms straight out sideways. *Chest*: touch chest. *Nut*: touch
head. *Tree*: stretch arms straight up. *Lines 3 & 4*: turn in place. *Variation*: 1. Say and perform as above. 2. Repeat verse, not saying word
chest, but performing all action. 3. Repeat verse, this time not saying
words *chest* and *nut*, but performing all actions. 4. Repeat verse, this time
not saying words *chest*, *nut*, and *tree*, but performing all actions.

Earth Goes Round

Earth is round;
Goes round and round.
Goes round and round;
Oh, earth is round.

— *Gloria T. Delamar.*

Lines 1 & 4: extend arms and form large circle by touching fingertips.
Lines 2 & 3: keeping arms in circle, turn in place.

The Brownies and the Owl

An owl sat alone on the branch of a tree,
And he was as quiet, as quiet could be.

'Twas night, and his eyes were open like this,
He looked all around, not a thing did he miss.

Some brownies climbed up the branch of the tree,
And they were as quiet, as quiet could be.
A wind came along and the branches swung,
The owl and the brownies tightly clung.

The owl said "Whoo," and fast as could be,
The brownies ran down to the foot of the tree.
The owl heard their footsteps pattering down,
And he flew away to another town.

—*Author unknown.*

VERSE 1 — *Lines 1 & 2*: stretch out arms to represent branches. *Lines 3 & 4*: circle both eyes with fingers and look around. VERSE 2 — *Lines 1 & 2*: stoop down, then run hands from feet all the way up sides of body until arms are outstretched again. *Lines 3 & 4*: sway arms and body. VERSE 3 — *Lines 1 & 2*: run fingers down sides of body to feet. *Lines 3 & 4*: flap arms for owl's wings and turn in place.

Tippy Toe

Tippy tippy, tip toe
See how we go
Tippy tippy tip toe
To and fro
Tippy tippy tip toe
Through the house
Tippy tippy tip toe
Like a mouse.

—*Author unknown.*

Lines 1, 3, 5, & 7: standing in place, tiptoe lightly with both feet. *Line 2*: hands to eyes. *Line 4*: hands out and back in. *Line 6*: tiptoe turning in place. *Line 8*: hunch down to floor.

Jack-in-the-Box

Jack-in-the-box all shut up tight
Not a breath of air, not a ray of light,
How dark it must be, he cannot see,
Open the box and up jumps he!

—*Author unknown.*

Lines 1, 2, & 3: stoop with hands on head. *Line 4*: lift hands and jump up.

Teddy Bear

Teddy Bear, Teddy Bear, turn around,
Teddy Bear, Teddy Bear, touch the ground,
Teddy Bear, Teddy Bear, go up stairs,
Teddy Bear, Teddy Bear, say your prayers,
Teddy Bear, Teddy Bear, turn out the light,
Teddy Bear, Teddy Bear, say good night.
        — *Old American rhyme.*

Perform all lines as described, and at last line, lay head on folded hands.

Johnny's Hammers

Johnny works with *one* hammer,
One hammer, one hammer,
Johnny works with one hammer,
Then he works with *two*.

Johnny works with *two* hammers,
Two hammers, two hammers,
Johnny works with two hammers,
Then he works with *three*.

Johnny works with *three* hammers,
Three hammers, three hammers,
Johnny works with three hammers,
Then he works with *four*.

Johnny works with *four* hammers,
Four hammers, four hammers,
Johnny works with *four* hammers,
Then he works with *five*.

Johnny works with *five* hammers,
Five hammers, five hammers,
Johnny works with five hammers,
Then he goes to *sleep*.
        — *Author unknown.*

Action — *One* hammer: pound right fist on right knee. *Two* hammers:

pound both fists on corresponding knees. *Three* hammers: tap right foot along with fists. *Four* hammers: tap both feet along with fists. *Five* hammers: move head back and forth along with other actions. *Sleep*: stop all actions and rest head on hands.

The Organ Grinder

The organ man, the organ man,
Is standing in the street.
His little monkey claps his hands,
And dances with his feet.
He throws his arms up in the air,
And round and round he winds,
He chatters and his master sings,
While the organ grinds.

— *Gloria T. Delamar*.

Lines 1 & 2: make fist of left hand and rotate right hand beside it in a circle as though turning the handle of a hand-organ. *Line 3*: clap. *Line 4*: move feet up and down. *Line 5*: throw arms up in air. *Line 6*: turn around. *Lines 7 & 8*: make motions of playing organ as in lines 1 & 2.

Little Teapot

I'm a little teapot,
Short and stout,
Here is my handle,
Here is my spout.
When I get all steamed up,
Then I shout,
Just tip me over,
And pour me out.

— *Author unknown*.

Lines 1 & 2: stoop. *Line 3*: put one elbow (hand on hip, elbow bent outward) for the handle. *Line 4*: pull other elbow close, raise forearm and point fingers outward for the spout. *Lines 5 & 6*: jump up. *Lines 7 & 8*: bend toward side which is the spout, as though pouring tea from it.

Ten Brave Firemen

Ten brave firemen,
Sleeping in a row.

Ding goes the bell,
Down the pole they go.
Off on the engine,
Oh, oh, oh.

This is the fire engine,
This is the hose.
The firemen work very fast,
When the siren blows.

Up goes the ladder
Out goes the hose,
The fire is out,
And that's the way it goes.
— *Author unknown.*

VERSE 1 — *Lines 1 & 2*: hold out hands with fingers curled. *Line 3*: put up hand and pull down as though pulling on a rope. *Line 4*: raise hands together and bring them down as though holding onto pole. *Lines 5 & 6*: turn around once. VERSE 2 — *Line 1*: indicate body. *Line 2*: extend right arm. *Lines 3 & 4*: step in place. VERSE 3 — *Line 1*: raise left arm. *Lines 2 & 3*: move right arm back and forth. *Line 4*: fold arms over chest.

Tap and Clap

Two little feet go tap, tap, tap.
Two little hands go clap, clap, clap.
A quick little leap up from the chair,
Two little arms reach high in the air.
Two little feet go jump, jump, jump.
Two little hands go thump, thump, thump.
One little baby turns round and round.
One little child sits quietly down.
— *Author unknown.*

Follow actions of verse as spoken.

My Monkey

I had a little monkey,
His name was Slimsy Jim.
I put him in a rowboat
And sent him out to swim.
He fell into the water.

He broke his wooly head.
And now my little monkey,
Is dead, dead, dead.

—Author unknown.

Lines 1 & 2: scratch under arms as monkey scratches. *Line 3:* make motions of rowing a boat. *Line 4:* make motions of swimming. *Line 5:* make diving motion with both hands. *Line 6:* hold head with both hands and shake head. *Line 7:* scratch again. *Line 8:* fold hands in lap.

Salute to the Captain

Salute to the Captain,
Bow to the King.
Turn around, turn around,
Here comes the Queen.

—Author unknown.

Line 1: salute. *Line 2:* bow. *Line 3:* turn around. *Line 4:* put hands on top of head to indicate crown.

The Farmer

First the farmer sows his seeds,
Then he stands and takes his ease,
He stamps his foot
And claps his hands,
And turns around to view his lands.

—Author unknown.

Line 1: shake hand as though sowing seeds. *Line 2:* stand still. *Line 3:* stamp foot. *Line 4:* clap hands. *Line 5:* turn around once.

Funny Duck

Waddle, waddle, waddle duck,
Waddle to the pond.
Paddle, paddle, paddle duck,
Paddle round and round.
Tail up, head down, funny little duck,
Tail up, head down, funny little duck.

—Author unknown.

Lines 1 & 2: flap arms at sides. *Lines 3 & 4*: make paddling movements with both hands. *Line 5*: put both hands behind back to represent duck tail, then bob head down. *Line 6*: repeat line five.

Two Little Apples

Way, way up in an apple tree
Two little apples smiled at me.
I shook that tree as hard as I could,
Down came those apples —
Ummmm, they were good.

— Author unknown.

Line 1: stretch hands high overhead. *Line 2*: clench both fists to represent apples. *Line 3*: shake body. *Line 4*: stoop to floor, putting fists on floor. *Line 5*: rub stomach to indicate having eaten apples.

Ticks and Tocks

The watch on my arm makes a little click,
Tick, tick, tick, tick, tick, tick, tick.

A different sound has the clock on the wall,
Tick tock, tick tock, is its call.

And in the hall the grandfather clock,
Says tock —— tock —— tock —— tock.

Tick, tick, tick, tick, tick, tick, tick.
Tick tock, tick tock, tick tock.
Tock —— tock —— tock —— tock.

— Gloria T. Delamar.

Line 1: make small circle with right index finger and thumb and hold it against left wrist. *Line 2*: raise right index finger and move it back and forth in time with the "tick, tick," which should be said rather fast. *Line 3*: using both hands, extended, make a circle joining index fingers together and thumbs together. *Line 4*: bend elbow with forearm raised and move forearm back and forth in time to "tick tock," which should be said at a moderate pace. *Line 5*: stand straight and frame face with hands. *Line 6*: keeping stiff, move back and forth from one foot to the other in time to "tock," which should be drawn out in a slow voice. *Line 7*: repeat line 2. *Line 8*: repeat line 4. *Line 9*: repeat line 6.

Spider Web

I'm a big spider,
I spin, I spin,
I spin big webs,
To catch little flies in.

—Author unknown.

Lines 1 & 3: hold up arms and open hands. *Line 2*: turn in place. *Line 4*: fold arms tightly to chest.

Jelly

Jelly on my head,
Jelly on my toes,
Jelly on my coat,
Jelly on my nose.

Laughing and a-licking,
Having me a time,
Jelly on my belly,
But I like it fine.

Jelly is my favorite food,
And when I'm in a jelly mood,
I can't ever get enough
Of that yummy, gummy stuff.

Pretty soon it will be spring,
And I'll do my gardening,
But I'll plant no flower-bed,
I'll plant jelly-beans instead.

—Author unknown.

VERSE 1 — *Line 1*: touch head. *Line 2*: touch toes. *Line 3*: touch chest. *Line 4*: touch nose. VERSE 2 — *Lines 1 & 2*: hold cheeks and shake head from side to side. *Lines 3 & 4*: rub tummy. VERSE 3 — *Lines 1, 2, & 3*: pretend to eat. *Line 4*: rub tummy. VERSE 4 — *Lines 1 & 2*: stoop and scratch at floor to indicate gardening. *Line 3*: get up, shake head "no." *Line 4*: rub tummy.

Born on Days

Monday's child is fair of face.
Tuesday's child is full of grace.

Wednesday's child is full of woe.
Thursday's child has far to go.
Friday's child is loving and giving.
Saturday's child works hard for a living.
But the child that is born on the Sabbath Day,
Is blythe and bonny and good and gay.
— *Old American rhyme.*

Line 1: preen in looking glass. *Line 2:* bow or curtsy. *Line 3:* rub eyes and cry. *Line 4:* walk. *Line 5:* bow and reach forward as though bestowing a gift on someone. *Line 6:* pretend to use a pick-axe. *Lines 7 & 8:* skip.

Good Night

Two little hands go clap, clap, clap,
Two little arms lie in my lap,
Two little feet go bump, bump, bump,
Two little legs give one big jump,
Two little eyes are shut up tight,
One little voice whispers low, "Good night."
— *Author unknown.*

Lines 1, 2, 3, 4, & 5: perform as verse indicates. *Line 6:* make flat pillow of hands to cradle head.

Me Complete

I have ten little fingers,
Ten little toes,
Two little arms,
And one little nose.
One little mouth,
And two little ears,
Two little eyes
For smiles and tears.
One little head,
And two little feet,
One little chin,
And that's me complete.
— *Author unknown.*

Touch each part with both hands as verse indicates.

Six Little Ducks

Six little ducks without a shoe
Big ducks, little ducks, pretty ones too,
But the one with the feathers curled up in the back
Led all the others with a quack, quack, quack.
They wiggled, and they wobbled as all ducks do,
Big ones, little ones, pretty ones too,
The one with the feathers curled up in the back,
Led all the others with a quack, quack, quack.

—Author unknown.

Line 1: point to feet. *Lines 2 & 6*: put arms wide for big, close for little, and wiggle hands for pretty. *Lines 3 & 7*: turn to show back and put hands behind back with fingers curled up. *Lines 4 & 8*: open and close one hand to indicate quacking. *Line 5*: put hands on hips and wobble body.

Rag Doll

Let's play rag doll,
Let's not make a sound.
Fling your arms and body
Loosely around.
Fling your arms and your feet,
And let your head go free,
Be the raggeyest, rag doll,
You ever did see.

—Author unknown.

Keep body very loose and perform as words indicate.

Grandfather, Grandmother Tat

Grandfather, Grandmother Tat,
Wave one hand like that.
Grandfather, Grandmother Tat,
Clap two hands like that.
Grandfather, Grandmother Tat,
Stamp two feet like that.
Grandfather, Grandmother Tat,
Nod their heads like that.
Funny old Grandfather,
Funny old Grandmother,
Sit back down like that.

—Author unknown.

Turn in place when saying "Grandfather, Grandmother Tat" and "Funny old, etc." Perform other lines as words indicate.

Snowman

Once there was a snowman
Stood outside the door,
Thought he'd like to come inside
And play about the floor.
Thought he'd like to warm himself
By the firelight red,
Thought he'd like to climb up
On the big white bed.

So he called to the North Wind
"Help me now, I pray,
I'm completely frozen,
Standing here this way."
So the North Wind came along
And blew him thru the door,
Now there's nothing left of him
But a puddle on the floor.

—Author unknown.

VERSE 1 — *Lines 1 & 2*: stand still, put arms forward and apart, representing frame of door. *Lines 3 & 4*: stoop to floor. *Lines 5 & 6*: rub hands together as though warming them before a fire. *Lines 7 & 8*: make climbing movements with legs. VERSE 2 — *Lines 1, 2, 3, & 4*: cup hands beside mouth to call North Wind. *Lines 5 & 6*: spin around. *Lines 7 & 8*: sink slowly to floor as snowman melts into a puddle.

If All the Seas

If all the seas were one sea,
What a **great** sea that would be!
And if all the trees were one tree,
What a **great** tree that would be!
And if all the axes were one axe,
What a **great** axe that would be!
And if all the men were one man,
What a **great** man that would be!

And if the **great** man
Took the **great** axe,

And cut down the **great** tree,
And let it fall into the **great** sea,
What a **splish-splash** that would be!
                        —*Mother Goose rhyme.*

VERSE 1—*Lines 1 & 2*: make a large circle with arms extended and hands touching. *Lines 3 & 4*: raise both arms. *Lines 5 & 6*: chop with right arm. *Lines 7 & 8*: touch own shoulders. VERSE 2—*Line 1*: touch own shoulders. *Line 2*: chop with right arm. *Line 3*: raise both arms. *Line 4*: make large circle of arms. *Line 5*: throw both arms up and jump up.

4. Holiday Potpourri

These seasonal verses are regular fingerplays, five-finger-plays, and more-than-finger-plays. Because they are for specific holidays, they have been grouped together for easy seasonal reference.

In general, there are very few traditional holiday verses usable as fingerplays. This section therefore contains a large number of original pieces written to fill that need.

Valentine's Day

A Valentine for Jill

Jack ran up to Jill's front door,
To leave a valentine for her.
He knocked upon the door and then,
He ran back down the street again.

Jill came out and looked around
And saw it lying on the ground.
She read the name signed on the back,
Then went running after Jack.
> — *Gloria T. Delamar.*

VERSE 1 — *Lines 1 & 2*: run up left arm with right fingers. *Line 3*: knock on left hand with right. *Line 4*: run back down left arm. VERSE 2 — *Lines 1 & 2*: look around and down with left hand. *Line 3*: hold left hand flat as though reading it. *Line 4*: run left hand to right hand.

Valentine Candy

The valentine Dad gave to Mom,
Was really very dandy,

69

We unwrapped it very fast,
'Cause it was chocolate candy.
— *Gloria T. Delamar.*

Line 1: hold up thumbs to indicate Dad and Mom. *Line 2*: clap at word "dandy." *Line 3*: roll hands around each other. *Line 4*: pretend to eat a piece of candy, then rub tummy.

This Valentine

This valentine is for bobble-dee-boo.
This valentine is for cobble-dee-coo.
This valentine is for dobble-dee-doo.
This valentine is for wobble-dee-woo.
And this valentine is special too,
Because this valentine is for yobble-dee-YOU.
— *Gloria T. Delamar.*

Five-finger-play.

My Valentine

One is for your heart so true,
Two is for the smile you do.
Three is for your wind-blown hair,
Four is for your cheeks so fair.
Five is for your eyes that shine,
Will you be my valentine?
— *Gloria T. Delamar.*

Five-finger-play.

Valentine Mail

One, two, three, four, five,
When will the valentines arrive?

Six, seven, eight, nine, ten,
When the postman comes again.
— *Gloria T. Delamar.*

Five-finger-play.

Easter

The Easter Rabbit's Habit

In a green and yellow basket
I found last Easter day,
I saw a purple egg
And jellybeans so gay.
And mother says he'll come again,
The little Easter rabbit,
With a basket, father says,
For that's his Easter habit.

— Gloria T. Delamar.

Lines 1 & 2: cup hands to form a basket. *Line 3*: touch index fingers together and thumbs together to form an oval to represent egg. *Line 4*: touch index finger to thumb on each hand to form two small ovals to represent jellybeans. *Lines 5 & 6*: with backs of wrists on top of head, point hands upward for rabbit's ears. *Lines 7 & 8*: cup hands to form a basket.

Some Things That Easter Brings

Easter duck and Easter chick,
Easter eggs with chocolate thick,
Easter hats for one and all;
Easter bunny makes a call!
Happy Easter always brings
Such a lot of pleasant things.

— Author unknown.

Line 1: for duck put both hands behind back and stick hands out with palms up (duck's tail). For chick, flap both arms at sides as though a chick were flapping its wings. *Line 2*: touch index finger to thumb on each hand to form two small ovals to represent eggs. *Line 3*: put hands on head with fingers touching making a little peak to indicate a hat. *Line 4*: with backs of wrists on top of head, raise hands to point upward to represent rabbit's ears. *Lines 5 & 6*: fold hands in lap.

Easter Bunny

Easter bunny hops along,
With wrinkled nose and ears so long,

In his basket blue and pink,
He has colored eggs, I think.
— *Gloria T. Delamar.*

Line 1: make hand hop in front of you. *Line 2*: point to nose, then put backs of wrists on head with hands sticking straight up for rabbit's long ears. *Line 3*: cup hands to form a basket. *Line 4*: make two egg shapes by putting index finger to thumb on each hand.

The Easter Rabbit's Ears

The Easter rabbit came one day,
And bent his ears way down this way.
He perked them up,
Then one went down,
And then he changed them both around.
Then both went up,
And off he hopped.
Hop, hop, hop, hop, hop.
— *Gloria T. Delamar.*

Line 1: put up right index and middle fingers for rabbit's ears. *Line 2*: bend ears down. *Line 3*: put ears up straight. *Line 4*: put down index finger. *Line 5*: put index finger up and middle finger down. *Line 6*: put ears straight up. *Lines 7 & 8*: hop hand. (This can easily be used at other than Easter time, simply by changing the words "Easter rabbit" to "little bunny.")

Coloring the Eggs

This bunny said, "I really think,
    I'm going to color my eggs pink."
This bunny said, "The best I've seen,
    Are eggs that are a grassy green."
This bunny said, "It's time you knew,
    I'm going to color my eggs blue."
This bunny said, "Well listen, fellow,
    My eggs are going to be bright yellow."
This bunny said with a shake of his head,
    "I'm going to color my eggs red."
— *Gloria T. Delamar.*

Five-finger-play.

The Easter Rabbit's Helpers

The Easter Rabbit's helpers, five in a row,
The first one said, "Is it time to go?"
The second one said, "The colored eggs are packed."
The third one said, "The jelly-beans are stacked."
The fourth one said, "The baskets are near!"
The fifth one said, "Why Easter-time is here!"
— *Gloria T. Delamar.*

Five-finger-play.

Other fingerplays suitable for Easter can be found elsewhere in this book: "Funny Duck" (page 62), "Jelly" (page 64), "Six Little Ducks" (page 66), "The Bunny's Hole" (page 35), and "This Bunny" (page 54).

Halloween

Making a Jack-o'-Lantern

On my Jack-o'-lantern
I will put great eyes,
They will be so big and round,
He'll look very wise.

And, of course, he'll have a nose
In the usual place,
Exactly in the middle
Of his bright orange face.

His teeth, with a knife
I'll have to cut in,
But I can't decide
If he should frown or grin.
— *Gloria T. Delamar*

VERSE 1 — *All lines*: draw small circles in air in front of eyes with index finger as though cutting eyes into a Jack-o'-lantern. VERSE 2 — *All lines*: touch nose with index finger. VERSE 3 — *Lines 1, 2 & 3*: pretend to cut jagged teeth in air in front of mouth. *Line 4*: pull lips with fingers into a frown and grin.

Mr. Pumpkin

Old Mr. Pumpkin
Hiding in a box,
Take off the top,
And out he pops.

—*Author unknown.*

Lines 1 & 2: make fist of right hand (thumb inside fist) and cover fist with left hand. *Line 3*: remove left hand to indicate removing top. *Line 4*: pop right thumb up from fist.

A Little Witch

A little witch in a pointed cap,
On my door went rap, rap, rap.
When I went to open it,
She was not there;
She was riding on a broomstick,
High up in the air.

—*Author unknown.*

Line 1: make cap on head with hands, fingertips touching. *Line 2*: pretend to rap at door. *Lines 3 & 4*: pretend to open door. *Lines 5 & 6*: put right fist on left wrist and make left arm fly.

Masquerade

I'll pretend on Halloween
That I'm a fancy king or queen,
Or with a tambourine to hit
I'll wear a gypsy's bright outfit.
Perhaps I'll be a pirate dread,
Or maybe a devil all in red.
But the next day, you will see,
Once again, I will be me.

—*Gloria T. Delamar.*

Lines 1 & 2: put hands on top of head to indicate crown. *Lines 3 & 4*: clap once with each line as though hitting a tambourine. *Line 5*: cross arms in front of body with hands touching opposite shoulders. *Line 6*: with hands on top of head raise index fingers to represent devil's horns. *Line 7*: point index finger. *Line 8*: point to self.

Five Jack-o'-Lanterns

Five little Jack-o'-lanterns sitting on a gate,
The first one said, "It's getting late,"
The second one said, "I heard a noise,"
The third one said, "It's just some boys,"
The fourth one said, "Let's run, let's run,"
The fifth one said, "Let's stay and have fun."
When OOO went the wind and blew out the light,
And away they ran on Halloween night.
                    —*Author unknown.*

Five-finger-play. At end, making running-away movements with hand.

Witch, Old Witch

Witch, old witch, how do you fly?
    On a broomstick going by.
Witch, old witch, what do you wear?
    Black old clothes and uncombed hair.
Witch, old witch, what do you eat?
    Little green bugs and pickled pig's feet.
Witch, old witch, what do you drink?
    Apple cider vinegar and midnight ink.
Witch, old witch, do you live in a house?
    I live in a haystack, with a little mouse.
                    —*Gloria T. Delamar.*

Five-finger-play.

Thanksgiving

Ten Fat Turkeys

Ten fat turkeys standing in a row.
They spread their wings and tails just so.
They strut to the left.
They strut to the right.
They all stand up ready to fight.
Along comes a man with a great big gun—
Bang! You should see those turkeys run!
                    —*Author unknown.*

Lines 1 & 2: hold up all ten fingers spread wide. *Line 3*: move hands in jumps to the left. *Line 4*: move hands in jumps to the right. *Line 5*: hold hands up. *Line 6*: extend right arm and put left hand under right elbow. *Line 7*: after "bang," both hands run to hide behind back.

Our Turkey

Our turkey is a big fat bird
He gobbles when he talks
His long red chin is drooping down
He waddles when he walks.
His tail is like a spreading fan
On Thanksgiving Day —
He spreads his tail high in the air
And whooooooooooosh — he flies away!
— *Author unknown.*

Line 1: hold hands far apart. *Line 2*: open and close one hand to indicate gobbling. *Line 3*: cup hand under chin. *Line 4*: move hands up and down alternately slightly apart. *Lines 5 & 6*: hold up and spread out fingers of one hand. *Lines 7 & 8*: shoot hand up into air.

Here Is a Turkey

Here is a turkey with his tail
    spread wide.
He sees the farmer coming
    so he's trying to hide.
He runs across the barnyard
    wobble, wobble, wobble.
Talking turkey talk
    gobble, gobble, gobble.
— *Author unknown.*

Line 1: hold up right hand with fingers spread. *Line 2*: advance left hand. *Line 3*: move right hand from side to side. *Line 4*: open and close right hand.

Five Little Pilgrims

Five little Pilgrims on Thanksgiving Day
The first one said, "I'll have cake if I may."
The second one said, "I'll have turkey roasted."

The third one said, "I'll have chestnuts toasted."
The fourth one said, "I'll have pumpkin pie."
The fifth one said, "Oh, cranberries I spy."
But before the Pilgrims ate their turkey dressing,
They bowed their heads and said a Thanksgiving blessing.
                              —*Author unknown.*

Five-finger-play.

Five Little Turkeys

Five little turkeys standing in a row
First little turkey said, "I don't want to grow."
Second little turkey said, "Why do you say that?"
Third little turkey said, "I want to get fat."
Fourth little turkey said, "Thanksgiving is near."
Fifth little turkey said, "Yes, that's what I hear."

Then the five little turkeys that were standing in a row
All said together, "Come on, let's GO!"
                              —*Author unknown.*

Five-finger-play.

Other fingerplays suitable for Thanksgiving can be found elsewhere in this book: "Big Indians" (page 18), "Indians and Trees" (page 19), "John Brown Had a Little Indian" (page 45), "Mr. Turkey and Mr. Duck" (page 23), "Ten Injuns" (page 50), and "Ten Little Indians" (page 19).

Christmas

Clap for Santa Claus

O, clap, clap the hands,
And sing with glee!
For Christmas is coming
And merry are we.

How swift o'er the snow
The tiny reindeer
Are trotting and bringing
Good Santa Claus near.

Our stockings we'll hang,
And while we're asleep,
Then down through the chimney
Will Santa Claus creep.

He'll empty his pack,
Then up he will come
And calling his reindeer,
Will haste away home.

Then clap, clap the hands!
And sing out with glee,
For Christmas is coming
And merry are we!

— *Emilie Poulsson.**

VERSE 1 — *All lines*: clap hands. VERSE 2 — *All lines*: lock thumbs together and make walking motions with other fingers to indicate reindeer and sleigh. VERSE 3 — *Lines 1 & 2*: point down with four fingers of one hand. *Lines 3 & 4*: put one fist on top of the other to represent chimney and put upper thumb inside of upper fist to represent Santa Claus going down chimney. VERSE 4 — *Lines 1 & 2*: raise thumb from upper fist as Santa Claus comes up chimney. *Lines 3 & 4*: lock thumbs and walk with fingers. VERSE 5 — *All lines*: clap hands.

Who Is Coming?

Who is coming down the chimney tonight,
With his coat all red,
And his beard all white?
He'll have a great big bag of toys
For all the little girls and boys.
He'll be laughing, that's because
He's the happy Santa Claus.

— *Gloria T. Delamar.*

Line 1: make downward motion with hand. *Line 2*: point to body. *Line 3*: put hands to chin for beard. *Lines 4 & 5*: put both hands over one shoulder as though holding bag. *Lines 6 & 7*: hold tummy and rock in laughing motion traditional to Santa Claus.

---

*Fingerplays for Nursery and Kindergarten, *Lothrop, Lee, & Shepard, Boston, 1893.*

Santa in the Chimney

Here's the chimney,
And here's the top,
Take off the cover,
Out Santa Claus pops.
—Author unknown.

Line 1: make fist of right hand. *Line 2*: cover with left hand. *Line 3*: remove left hand. *Line 4*: pop up right thumb.

Santa and His Sleigh

Here is old Santa,
Here is his sleigh.
These are the reindeer
Which he drives away.
Dasher, Dancer, Prancer, Vixen,
Comet, Cupid, Donner, Blitzen.
Ho, ho, ho,
Away they all go!
—Author unknown.

Line 1: hold up right thumb. *Line 2*: hold up left thumb. *Lines 3 & 4*: show eight fingers. *Lines 5 & 6*: bob a finger at each name. *Lines 7 & 8*: lock thumbs and run fingers in front and away.

Santa's Gifts

Santa Claus will soon be here,
Bringing gifts for Christmas cheer.
Father wants a reel for fish.
Mother wants a pretty dish.
Brother wants a basketball.
Sister wants a crying doll.
Baby wants some blocks of wood,
So we will all be very good.
—Gloria T. Delamar.

Line 3: make circular motions around one fist with other hand to indicate a reel. *Line 4*: cup hands to form a dish. *Line 5*: make a ball with both hands. *Line 6*: pretend to hold doll in arms and rock it. *Line 7*: place one fist on the other. *Line 8*: fold hands in lap. It can also be a five-finger-play.

Ten Little Pine Trees

Ten little pine trees,
Standing in a wood.
Waiting for the woodsman,
To chop them down for good.
    Chop, chop, chop, chop, chop —
    Chop, chop, chop, chop, chop!

Ten little pine trees,
Waiting for the day,
Waiting for the people
To come haul them away.
    You, you, you, you, you —
    You, you, you, you, you!

Dressed in lights and garlands,
Ten green pines do please;
In ten different houses,
They are Christmas trees.
    One, two, three, four, five —
    six, seven, eight, nine, ten!
            — *Gloria T. Delamar.*

Five-finger-play. Hold up both hands. Fold fingers down one by one at each "chop." Put fingers back up one by one at each "you." Count each finger for numbers.

Ten Things That Mean Christmas

Christmas is a happy time;
It's the time for *bells* to chime;
It's the time for lighted *trees*;
It's the time for *gifts* that please;
It's the time for *mistletoe*;
It's the time for falling *snow*.
Christmas time is many things:
It's the time for *carol*-sings;
It's the time for *candle*-making;
It's the time for *cookie*-baking;
It's the time for dark green *holly*;
And it's the time for *Santa* jolly.
            — *Gloria T. Delamar.*

Five-finger-play.

Five Little Reindeer

Five little reindeer, standing in a row,
The first one said, "Oh, hear the wind blow."
The second one said, "It's going to snow."
The third one said, "Oh, I hope so."
The fourth one said, "It will, I know."
The fifth one said, "Where did Santa go?"
Then Santa came out and said, "Ho, ho, ho."
— *Gloria T. Delamar*.

Five-finger-play.

Five Christmas Bells

Five merry bells at Christmas time;
The first bell said, "I'm going to chime."
The second bell said, "I'm going to bong."
The third bell said, "I'll say ding-dong."
The fourth bell said, "I'm going to ting."
The fifth bell said, "I'll clap and sing."
One, two, three, four, five — oh hear —
The bells ring out their Christmas cheer.
— *Gloria T. Delamar*.

Five-finger-play. After counting off 1 to 5, turn hand so fingers point toward floor. Swing hand to represent ringing bells.

The Toy Shop

Here is the toy shop
And happy are we
For this is the good toyman's shop that we see.
So many, many toys
All in a row
And bright colored tops
That sing as they go.
And here in a box
Is a doll that can talk
And here is a black wooly dog
That can walk.
Just see this funny old
Jack in the box,

Watch him pop out
Oh my, what a shock!
Here is the counter
Piled high with the toys,
For you little girls
And you, little boys.
Here is the toyman
And here is his clerk
To sell all those toys
How hard they must work.
Now gently close
The toy shop door
And look at the toys
In the window once more.
We hope, little toys,
That some of you may
Come straight to us
On glad Christmas day.

—*Author unknown.*

More-than-finger-play. Actions — *Toy Shop*: make roof overhead with hands. *Top*: turn in place. *Doll*: keeping stiff, rock sideways from foot to foot. *Dog*: stoop down to put hands on floor. *Jack-in-box*: jump up. *Counter*: extend arms, bend elbows, put fingertips together to form a counter. *Toyman*: one hand. *Clerk*: other hand. *Door*: place hands slowly flat together in prayer position. *Window*: make window, thumbs touching and index fingers touching.

5. Join-In Rhythms

Join-in rhythms are also called choral speeches, choral responses, or responsive readings. What makes them different from other verses is that they are performed by more than one person. There are always at least two parts, usually divided into a leader and the group refrain or response. Other divisions can also be made, such as two people, or two groups, or a leader and several groups, or even several leaders with several groups. The refrains of join-in rhythms are interesting because they teach performers how the same word or phrase can show a different meaning or emotion in response to certain words. Through the use of tonal quality (loud, soft, quick, slow) or different sounds (notes that rise or fall) a story is told. Join-in rhythms are good for experiences in sharing poetry and also for "performing." They make excellent material for short, easy-to-learn dramatic presentations.

John Cook

John Cook, had a little grey mare.
    Hee haw hum.   (IN CHANTING TONES)
Her back stood up and her bones were bare.
    Hee haw hum.   (FASTER CHANT)
John Cook was riding up Shooter's Bank.
    Hee haw hum.   (IN ASCENDING TONES)
And there his nag did kick and prank.
    Hee haw hum.   (MAKE WORDS SOUND AS KICKS)
John Cook was riding up Shooter's Hill.
    Hee haw hum.   (ASCENDING TONES)
His mare fell down and made her will.
    Hee haw hum.   (DESCENDING TONES)
The bridle and saddle were laid on the shelf.
    Hee haw hum.   (SADLY)
If you want any more you may sing it yourself.
    Hee haw hum.   (SASSILY)
                                 —*Author unknown.*

The Chee-Choo Bird

A little green bird sat on a fence rail.
    Chee-choo, chee-choo, chee-choo.   (GAILY)
The song was the sweetest I ever heard.
    Chee-choo, chee-choo, chee-choo.   (SONGLIKE)
I ran for some salt to put on his tail.
    Chee-choo, chee-choo, chee-choo.   (MENACING)
But while I was gone, away flew the bird.
    Chee-choo, chee-choo, chee-choo.   (HAPPILY)
                          —Author unknown.

Two Cats of Kilkenny

There once were two cats of Kilkenny.
Each thought there was one cat too many.
    Meow!   (SLIGHTLY SUSPICIOUS)
So they fought and they fit,
They scratched and they bit.
    Meow!   (ANGRILY)
'Til except for their nails,
And the tips of their tails,
    Meow!   (QUIETLY)
Instead of two cats,
There weren't any!   (SILENCE)
                       —Adapted from Mother Goose.

Grandfather Frog

A Grandfather Frog sat down on a stone.
    Gunk-gunk-gunk.
Croaking a song, he sat there alone.
    Gunk-gunk-gunk.
Along came a fly and said, "Mister Frog,
Hop over and catch me, here on my log."
    Gunk-gunk-gunk.
But Grandfather Frog just sat on his stone.
    Gunk-gunk-gunk.
Thinking and croaking, he sat there alone.
    Gunk-gunk-gunk.
So the foolish young fly flew away from his log,
And was caught on the tongue of Grandfather Frog.
    Gunk-gunk-gunk.
                    —Author unknown.

Twitter Whoo

The owl among the bushes sat,
The rain was soaking through his hat.
But when it dried, he said, "Oh quash,
It's all the better for the wash."
  Twitter whoo, twitter whoo,
  We'll do as other people do.

The owl perched on a mossy wall,
And soon began to hoot and call.
The moon appeared, he flapped his wing,
He said, "She comes to hear me sing."
  [Refrain.]

The owl stood in the dark of night,
There was no other thing in sight.
He said, "There's nothing here to do,
Except to twitter and to whoo."
  [Refrain.]

                    —*Author unknown.*

Donkey Darling Don

There was a funny donkey, once,
Whose name was Darling Don.
  Hee haw, hee haw, hee haw.   (HAPPILY)

He liked to run and wander,
From hither and to yon.
  Hee haw, hee haw, hee haw.   (PLAYFULLY)

He loved to run up Berry Hill,
At the edge of Berry Town.
  Hee haw, hee haw, hee haw.   (ASCENDING TONES)

And once he got up to the top,
He'd turn and clatter down.
  Hee haw, hee haw, hee haw.   (DESCENDING TONES)

He'd prance right up to Auntie Jess,
And nuzzle at her cheek.
  Hee haw, hee haw, hee haw.   (SLOWLY RUN TOGETHER)

Or stop beside old Grandpa True,
To give his coat a tweak.
  Hee haw, hee haw, hee haw.   (EACH WORD CLIPPED SHORT)

He'd hear the bell at recess time,
And hurry to the school.
  Hee haw, hee haw, hee haw.   (QUICKLY)

The boys and girls would cheer at him,
For clowning like a fool.
  Hee haw, hee haw, hee haw.   (FOOLISHLY)

His master, Farmer Theobald,
Would look for him all day.
  Hee haw, hee haw, hee haw.   (TAUNTINGLY)

But know the folks of Berry Town,
Liked Darling Don to play.
  Hee haw, hee haw, hee haw.   (LOVINGLY)

He'd never hurt or break a thing,
Nor cause a soul to weep.
  Hee haw, hee haw, hee haw.   (SOLEMNLY)

And at night Darling Don like everyone else,
Went quietly to sleep.
  Hee haw, hee haw, hee haw.   (SLEEPILY)
                                   — *Gloria T. Delamar.*

Cats and Cats' Meows

Little kittens softly say,
  Meow, Meow, Meow.   (SOFTLY, WEAKLY)
Mother cats with love say,
  Meow, meow, meow.   (LOVINGLY)
Big tom cats cry out,
  Meow, meow, meow.   (LOUDLY)
And wild cats scream about,
  Meow, meow, meow!   (WILDLY AND LOUDLY)
                                   — *Gloria T. Delamar.*

Grasshopper Green

Grasshopper Green is a comical chap,
He lives on the best of fare.

Bright little trousers, jacket, and cap,
These are his summer wear.
Out in the meadow he loves to go,
Playing in the sun.
    It's hopperty, skipperty, high and low,
    Summer's the time for fun.

Grasshopper Green has a dozen wee boys,
And as soon as their legs are strong,
Each of them joins in his frolicsome joys,
Singing his merry song.
Under the hedge they love to go
As soon as the day has begun.
    [Refrain.]

Grasshopper Green has a quaint little house,
It's under the hedge so gay,
Grandmother spider, as still as a mouse,
Watches him over the way.
Gladly he's calling the children, I know,
Out in the beautiful sun.
    [Refrain.]
                  —Author unknown.

The Mischievous Raven

A farmer went trotting upon his gray mare,
    Bumpety, bumpety, bump!   (BUMPILY)
With his daughter behind him, so rosy and fair,
    Lumpety, lumpety, lump!   (GAILY)
A raven cried "Croak," and they all tumbled down,
    Bumpety, bumpety, bump!   (DESCENDING TONES)
The mare broke her knees, and the farmer his crown,
    Lumpety, lumpety, lump!   (SADLY)
The mischievous raven flew laughing away,
    Bumpety, bumpety, bump!   (LAUGHINGLY)
And vowed he would serve them the same the next day,
    Lumpety, lumpety, lump!   (MISCHIEVOUSLY)
                  —Mother Goose rhyme.

The Cuckoo Is a Clever Bird

The cuckoo is a clever bird,
    Cuckoo, cuckoo.   (LILTING)
And seven wives he keeps, I've heard,
    Cuckoo, cuckoo.   (WHISPERING)

The first one sweeps and cleans all day,
The second one takes the dust away.
  Cuckoo, cuckoo.   (BRISKLY)
The third one scrubs the table bright,
And decks it with a cloth so white.
  Cuckoo, cuckoo.   (BRISKLY)
The fourth one brings him bread and wine,
The fifth one then with him will dine.
  Cuckoo, cuckoo.   (BRISKLY)
The sixth one makes his nest so warm,
The seventh sleeps there on his arm.
  Cuckoo, cuckoo.   (SOFTLY)
The cuckoo is a clever bird,
For seven wives he keeps, I've heard.
  Cuckoo, cuckoo, cuckoo.   (LILTING)
                    —*Author unknown.*

Oh Colly, My Cow

A story, a sad one, I'll tell you just now;
Its all about selling of Colly, my cow.
  Ah sweet, pretty Colly, oh Colly, my cow.
  Poor Colly will give no more milk to me now!

Said little Tom Tinker, "Pray, what do you mean,
By selling your Colly when she is so lean?"
  [Refrain.]

Then came the old tanner with whip at his side;
He bid me three shillings for Colly, my pride.
  [Refrain.]

The skin of my Colly was softer than silk;
And three times a day did my Colly give milk.
  [Refrain.]

The sound of her mooing was sweet and so low;
And how I do miss her you never shall know.
  [Refrain.]

Then good-bye, dear Colly, she's gone past recall;
She's sold to the tanner, her horns, head and all.
  [Refrain.]
                    —*Author unknown.*

The refrain should be chanted in a mock serious tone.

Little Grey Billy-Goat

Grandmother had a little grey billy-goat,
    Dinkums, dunkums, little grey billy-goat. (MATTER-OF-FACTLY)
Granny was fond of her little grey billy-goat,
    Dinkums, dunkums, little grey billy-goat. (FONDLY)
Little grey billy-goat thought he'd go awalking,
    Dinkums, dunkums, little grey billy-goat. (BRISKLY)
Big, grey wolves came stalking, astalking,
    Dinkums, dunkums, little grey billy-goat. (STEALTHILY)
All that was found was his hoofs and his horns,
    Dinkums, dunkums, little grey billy-goat. (SADLY)
Grandmother sits by the fire and mourns,
    Dinkums, dunkums, little grey billy-goat. (VERY QUIETLY)
                — *Russian folk rhyme.*

A Goblin Lives in Our House

        A goblin lives in our house, in our house, in our house.
        A goblin lives in our house all the year round.
He bumps
        And he jumps
                And he thumps
                        And he stumps.
He knocks
        And he rocks
                And he rattles at the locks.
        A goblin lives in our house, in our house, in our house.
        A goblin lives in our house all the year round.
        — *French folk rhyme.*

The Owl

An owl perched at night
In the branch of a tree.
    Whoo, whoo.   (MODERATELY)

He was watching the stars
In the sky, quietly.
    Whoo, whoo.   (WHISPER)

Far off in the woods
He could hear a slight noise.
    Whoo, whoo.   (SOFTLY, QUESTIONINGLY)

Then, voices came closer;
Some girls and some boys.
   Whoo, whoo.   (CLEARLY)

He could hear someone say,
"I'm not afraid here."
   Whoo, whoo.   (TWO TONES, DESCENDING)

And another voice answered,
"There's nothing to fear."
   Whoo, whoo.   (TWO TONES, ASCENDING)

And the owl quite agreed,
And wanted to say...
   Whoo, whoo.   (HOOTING)

His greeting was meant
In the friendliest way.
   Whoo, whoo.   (SOFTLY)

The group heard the hoot;
To them it held dread...
   Whoo, whoo.   (LOUDLY)

Coming at night
From the tree overhead.
   Whoo, whoo.   (DRAWN-OUT)

So they ran back home,
As fast as could be.
   Whoo, whoo.   (QUICKLY)

And the owl sat alone,
In the branch of the tree.
   Whoo, whoo.   (QUIETLY)
                                   — *Gloria T. Delamar.*

The Pie

Who made the pie?
   I did.   (MATTER-OF-FACTLY)
Who stole the pie?
   He did.   (ACCUSINGLY)
Who found the pie?
   She did.   (PROUDLY)

Who ate the pie?
You did. (SADLY)
Who cried for pie?
We all did. (WITH DESPAIR)
— *Author unknown.*

Pop-Pop-Popcorn

Yellow kernels we will take
With melted butter, for to make,
Pop-Pop-Popcorn.
Small and hard, not good to eat,
Look what happens in the heat,
Pop-Pop-Popcorn.
The kernels hop about the pot,
Bursting open, when they're hot,
Pop-Pop-Popcorn.
When the lid comes off, we see,
White and fluffy as can be,
Pop-Pop-Popcorn.
— *Gloria T. Delamar.*

Clapping of hands can accompany spoken refrains, to imitate popping of corn.

I Saw a Little Bird

Once I saw a little bird, come hop,
Hop, hop. (JUMPILY)
So I cried "little bird, will you stop,
Stop, stop." (BEGGING)
I was going to the window to say "Howdy-do,
Howdy-do." (FRIENDLY)
But he shook his little tail, and away he flew,
Flew, flew, away he flew. (AIRILY)
— *Mother Goose rhyme.*

The Cat and the Mice

The cat is asleep, she can't hear a sound,
The mice can come out and run around.
Skittery-skattery, skittery-skattery, (PLAYFULLY)
Skittery-skattery, skittery-skattery.

The cat is awake, she hears the mice play,
But the mice perk their ears, they hear the cat say;
    Meow!   (LOUDLY)

The mice run away, to hide in their holes,
So the cat can't reach them with her paws.
    Skittery-skattery, skittery-skattery,   (ALARMED)
    Skittery-skattery, skittery-skattery.

The mice are hidden away very deep,
So the cat stretches out, and goes back to sleep.
    Meow.   (SLEEPILY)
                     —*Author unknown.*

How to Treat a Horse

Uphill; spare me, spare me.
    Clippety-clop-clop.   (ASCENDING TONES)
Down hill; forbear me, forbear me.
    Clippety-clop-clop.   (DESCENDING TONES)
Riding along; spare me not.
    Clippety-clop-clop.   (QUICKLY)
But let me not drink when I am hot.
    Clippety-clop-clop.   (DRAWN-OUT)
Or I'll drop over on the spot.
    Clippety-clop-clop!   (DROP VOICE AT LAST 'CLOP')
                     —*Author unknown.*

How Folks Ride

This is the way the ladies ride;
    Nim, nim, nim.   (DAINTILY)
This is the way the ladies ride;
    Nim, nim, nim, trimmy-trim.
This is the way the gentlemen ride;
    Trot, trot, trot.   (BRISKLY)
This is the way the gentlemen ride;
    Trot, trot, trot, trot-along.
This is the way the huntsmen ride;
    Gallop, gallop, gallop.   (ENERGETICALLY)
This is the way the huntsmen ride;
    Gallop, gallop, gallop, tally-ho.
This is the way the farmers ride;
    Hobbledy hoy, hobbledy hoy.   (CAREFULLY)

This is the way the farmers ride;
   Hobbledy hoy, hobbledy hoy, hobbledy-gee.
This is the way the ploughboys ride;
   Plod, plod, plod.   (SLOWLY)
This is the way the ploughboys ride;
   Plod, plod, plod, puddle-plod.
This is the way the racers ride;
   With a whoosh, with a whoosh.   (QUICKLY)
This is the way the racers ride;
   With a whoosh, with a whoosh, with-the-wind.
This is the way the children ride;
   Gidday-up, gidday-up.   (PLAYFULLY)
This is the way the children ride;
   Gidday-up, gidday-up, whoa-whoa-whoa.
                     — Mother Goose rhyme.

How We Go

Here we go
   Up, up, up.   (ASCENDING TONES)
Here we go
   Down, down, down.   (DESCENDING TONES)
Here we go
   Ever so softly.   (SAY 'SOFTLY' SOFTLY)
Here we go
   Ever so loudly.   (SAY 'LOUDLY' LOUDLY)
Here we go
   Round, round, round, round,   (DIZZILY)
   Round, round, round.

                 — Gloria T. Delamar.

The Light-Hearted Fairy

Oh, who is so merry, so merry, heigh ho!
As the light-hearted fairy? Heigh ho, heigh ho!
He dances and sings
To the sound of his wings,
   With a hey, and a heigh, and a ho!

Oh, who is so merry, so airy, heigh ho!
As the light-hearted fairy? Heigh ho, heigh ho!
His nectar he sips
From the primroses' lips,
   With a hey, and a heigh, and a ho!

Oh, who is so merry, so merry, heigh ho!
As the light-hearted fairy? Heigh ho, heigh ho!
The night is his noon
And the sun is his moon,
With a hey, and a heigh, and a ho!
—*Author unknown.*

In a Castle Sat a Maid

In a castle sat a maid.
    Ding, dong, ding, ding, dong,   (HAPPILY)
    All among the roses.
A knight rode by to serenade.
    Ding, dong, ding, ding, dong,   (SING-SONG)
    All among the roses.
A wall was there. The wall was high.
    Ding, dong, ding, ding, dong,   (FORBIDDINGLY)
    All among the roses.
He could hear the maiden sigh.
    Ding, dong, ding, ding, dong,   (SADLY)
    All among the roses.
The wall it made a barricade.
    Ding, dong, ding, ding, dong,   (STOUTLY)
    All among the roses.
The knight would hasten to her aid.
    Ding, dong, ding, ding, dong,   (DETERMINED)
    All among the roses.
He would break down half the wall.
    Ding, dong, ding, ding, dong.   (FIRMLY)
    All among the roses.
And yet more wall would have to fall.
    Ding, dong, ding, ding, dong,   (LOUDER)
    All among the roses.
He broke it down upon the ground.
    Ding, dong, ding, ding, dong,   (WITH FINALITY)
    All among the roses.
He searched until the maid was found.
    Ding, dong, ding, ding, dong.   (SLOWLY, SEARCHING)
    All among the roses.
Married were the knight and maid.
    Ding, dong, ding, ding, dong,   (BELL-LIKE, HAPPILY)
    All among the roses.
In the castle garden's shade.
    Ding, dong, ding, ding, dong,   (SOFTLY)
    All among the roses.
—*Author unknown.*

Aiken Drum

There was a man lived in the moon,
And his name was Aiken Drum.
And he played upon a ladle,
And his name was Aiken Drum.
His hat was made of ripe green cheese,
And he played upon a ladle,
And his name was Aiken Drum.
His coat was made of rare roast beef,
And he played upon a ladle,
And his name was Aiken Drum.
His buttons were made of penny loaves,
And he played upon a ladle,
And his name was Aiken Drum.
His vest was made of crusts of pie,
And he played upon a ladle,
And his name was Aiken Drum.
His pants were made of haggis bags,
And he played upon a ladle,
And his name was Aiken Drum.
His shoes were made of old tin cans,
And he played upon a ladle,
And his name was Aiken Drum.
There was a man lived in the moon,
And his name was Aiken Drum.

— *Old Scottish rhyme.*

Over the Hills and a Great Way Off

Tom he was a piper's son,
He learned to play when he was young,
But all the tune that he could play
Was "Over the hills and far away."
Over the hills and a great way off,
The wind shall blow my top-knot off.

Tom with his pipe did make such a noise,
That he pleased both the girls and boys.
They all danced while he did play
"Over the hills and far away."
[Refrain.]

Tom with his pipe did play with such skill,
That those who heard him could never keep still.

As soon as he played they began for to dance,
Even pigs on their hind legs would after him prance.
    [Refrain.]

As Dolly was milking her cow one day,
Tom took his pipe and began for to play.
So Doll and the cow danced "The Cheshire Round,"
Till the pail was broken and the milk ran on the ground.
    [Refrain.]

He met old Dame trot with a basket of eggs,
He used his pipe and she used her legs.
She danced about till the eggs were all broke,
She began for to fret, but he laughed at the joke.
    [Refrain.]

Tom saw a cross fellow was beating an ass,
Heavy laden with pots, pans, dishes and glass.
He took out his pipe and played them a tune,
And the poor donkey's load was lightened full soon.
    [Refrain.]
                  — *Old Scottish rhyme.*

The Man with the Gun

There was a little man,
And he had a little gun,
And his bullets were made of
    Lead, lead, lead.
He went to a brook,
And saw a little duck,
And shot it through the
    Head, head, head.
He carried it home,
To his old wife Joan,
And bade her a fire to
    Make, make, make.
To roast the little duck,
He had shot in the brook,
While he went to get the
    Drake, drake, drake.
The drake was a-swimming,
With his curly tail,
The little man made it his
    Mark, mark, mark.

He let off his gun,
But he fired too soon,
And the drake flew away with a
   Quack, quack, quack.
                    — Mother Goose rhyme.

The Keeper

The Keeper would a-hunting go,
And under his coat he carried a bow,
All for to shoot at a merrie little doe,
   Among the leaves so green-o!

The first doe he shot at he missed;
The second doe he trimmed, he kissed;
The third doe went where nobody wist;
   Among the leaves so green-o!

The fourth doe she did cross the plain;
The Keeper fetched her back again;
Where she is now she may remain;
   Among the leaves so green-o!

The fifth doe she did cross the brook;
The Keeper fetched her back with his crook;
Where she is now you must go and look;
   Among the leaves so green-o!
                    — Old English rhyme.

Three Acres of Land

My father left me three acres of land,
   Sing ivy, sing ivy;
My father left me three acres of land,
   Sing holly, go whistle and ivy!

I plowed it with a ram's horn,
   Sing ivy, sing ivy;
And sowed it all with one peppercorn,
   Sing holly, go whistle and ivy!

I harrowed it with brambles five,
   Sing ivy, sing ivy;
And reaped it with my pocketknife,
   Sing holly, go whistle and ivy!

I tied it up with purple yarn,
    Sing ivy, sing ivy;
And got the mice to carry it to the barn,
    Sing holly, go whistle and ivy!

I thrashed it with a goose's quill,
    Sing ivy, sing ivy;
And got the cat to carry it to the mill,
    Sing holly, go whistle and ivy!

My father left me three acres of land,
    Sing ivy, sing ivy;
My father left me three acres of land,
    Sing holly, go whistle and ivy!
                    — *Author unknown.*

Old Roger

Old Roger is dead and laid in his grave,
    Laid in his grave, laid in his grave.
Old Roger is dead and laid in his grave,
    Aha! Laid in his grave.

They planted an apple tree over his head,
    Over his head, over his head.
They planted an apple tree over his head,
    Aha! Over his head.

The apples grew ripe and ready to fall,
    Ready to fall, ready to fall.
The apples grew ripe and ready to fall,
    Aha! Ready to fall.

There came an old woman to pick them all,
    To pick them all, to pick them all.
There came an old woman to pick them all,
    Aha! To pick them all.

Old Roger jumped up and gave her a knock,
    Gave her a knock, gave her a knock.
Old Roger jumped up and gave her a knock,
    Aha! Old Roger gave her a knock.

It made the old woman go hippety-hop,
    Go hippety-hop, go hippety-hop.

It made the old woman go hippety-hop,
Aha! Go hippety-hop.

Old Roger they say is buried and dead,
Buried and dead, buried and dead.
Old Roger they say is buried and dead,
Aha! Buried and dead.
— *Old English rhyme.*

Five Fools in a Barrow

Five fools in a barrow rode into Harrow,
Tra-la, tra-la, tra-la-la.

They boomped and they bumped and they limped
and they lumped,
And the faster they rumbled the faster they tumbled,
Tra-la, tra-la, tra-la-la.

Five fools in a barrow rode into Harrow,
Tra-la, tra-la, tra-la-la.

The wheels were just crust and covered with rust,
The barrow went bust and they fell in the dust,
Ha-ha, ha-ha, a-ha-ha!
— *Old English rhyme.*

The Carrion Crow

A carrion crow sat in an oak,
Derry, down derry, heigh-ho.
Watching a tailor shape his cloak;
Heigh-ho, the carrion crow,
Derry, down derry, heigh-ho.
Oh, wife, bring me my old bent bow,
Derry, down derry, heigh-ho.
That I may shoot yon carrion crow;
Heigh-ho, the carrion crow,
Derry, down derry, heigh-ho.
The tailor shot, and missed his mark,
Derry, down derry, heigh-ho.
And shot his own sow through the heart;
Heigh-ho, the carrion crow,
Derry, down derry, heigh-ho.

Oh, wife, bring brandy in a spoon,
Derry, down derry, heigh-ho.
For our old sow is in a swoon;
Heigh-ho, the carrion crow,
Derry, down derry, heigh-ho.
The tailor and wife saw the old sow croak,
Derry, down derry, heigh-ho.
While the carrion crow cawed in the oak;
Heigh-ho, the carrion crow,
Derry, down derry, heigh-ho.
Oh, derry, down derry, heigh-ho.
                    — *Mother Goose rhyme.*

The refrains should be chanted in a sing-song rhythm, to give the effect of a spoken tale with a rhythmic background.

The Bells of London Town

Gay go up, and gay go down,
To ring the bells of London town.

Oranges and lemons,
Say the bells of Saint Clement's.
Oranges and lemons.

Pancakes and fritters,
Say the bells of Saint Peter's.
Pancakes and fritters.

Two sticks and an apple,
Say the bells of Whitechapel.
Two sticks and an apple.

Bull's eyes and targets,
Say the bells of Saint Margaret's.
Bull's eyes and targets.

Brickbats and tiles,
Say the bells of Saint Giles.
Brickbats and tiles.

Pokers and tongs,
Say the bells of Saint John's.
Pokers and tongs.

Kettles and pans,
Say the bells of Saint Ann's.
   Kettles and pans.

Maids in white aprons,
Say the bells of Saint Catherine's.
   Maids in white aprons.

Old Father Baldpate,
Say the slow bells of Aldgate.
   Old Father Baldpate.

Half-pence and farthings,
Say the bells of Saint Martin's.
   Half-pence and farthings.

You owe me ten shillings,
Say the bells of Saint Helen's.
   You owe me ten shillings.

When will you pay me?
Say the bells of Old Bailey.
   When will you pay me?

When I grow rich,
Say the bells of Shoreditch.
   When I grow rich.

Pray, when will that be?
Say the bells of Stepney.
   Pray, when will that be?

I am sure I don't know,
Says the great bell at Bow.
   I am sure I don't know.

Here comes a candle to light you to bed,
And here comes a chopper to chop off your head.
   Here comes a candle to light you to bed,
   And here comes a chopper to chop off your head.
        — Mother Goose rhyme.

Each refrain should be intoned in a bell-like way. The final word of each
phrase should be held in a ringing tone.

Learning My Alphabet

I can start the alphabet;
   A, B, C!
But the middle I forget;
   Golly, gee!
I furl my brow and sadly fret;
   Woe is me!
It makes me feel badly upset;
   Not full of glee.
It makes me feel so much beset;
   Thinking...see?
I try and try the rest to get;
   What can it be?
As for the end, I know it yet;
   X, Y, Z!
Well, I know SOME of the alphabet;
   Hurray for me!

                    — *Gloria T. Delamar.*

The Circus Is Coming to Town

   The circus is coming to town —
There'll be a long parade;
   The circus is coming to town —
There'll be pink lemonade.
   The circus is coming to town —
There'll be a big brass band;
   The circus is coming to town —
There'll be a pop-corn stand.
   The circus is coming to town —
There'll surely be a clown;
   The circus is coming to town —
With a clown and merry-go-round.
   The circus is coming to town —
There's a dog and pony show;
   The circus is coming to town —
Let's go...
Let's go...
   Let's go.

                    — *Louise Abney.* *

If a different individual recites each of the lines telling what is included in the circus, the effect of a crowd anticipating the parade is enhanced.

*Choral Speaking Arrangements for the Upper Grades, *Expression Co., Mass., 1937, 1952.*

The Shoemaker

As I was walking along the way,
I looked in the shoemaker's window today.
With a rack-a-tack-tack and a rack-a-tack-too.

He was old and bent and feeble, too,
And as I watched, he made a shoe.
With a rack-a-tack-tack and a rack-a-tack too.

This was the way he made the shoe;
Busy with the leather his fingers flew.
With a rack-a-tack-tack and a rack-a-tack too.

With a sharp-pointed awl he made a hole,
Right through the upper and then through the sole.
With a rack-a-tack-tack and a rack-a-tack too.

He put in a peg, then he put in two,
And then with a smile he hammered it through.
With a rack-a-tack-tack and a rack-a-tack too.
                    —*Author unknown.*

The Man in the Moon

The man in the moon as he sails the sky,
Is a very remarkable skipper...
   Is a very remarkable skipper. (KNOWINGLY)
But he made a mistake when he tried to take,
A drink of milk from the dipper...
   A drink of milk from the dipper. (DOUBTFULLY)
He dipped right into the Milky Way,
And slowly and carefully filled it...
   And slowly and carefully filled it. (SLOWLY)
The Big Bear growled, and the Little Bear howled,
And scared him so he spilled it...
   And scared him so he spilled it. (WITH FINALITY)
                    —*Author unknown.*

Jeremiah Obadiah

Jeremiah Obadiah,
   Puff, puff, puff. (BREATHILY)

When he give his messages goes
> *Snuff, snuff, snuff.*   (SNIFFLY)

When he goes to school by day, he
> *Roars, roars, roars.*   (LOUDLY)

When he goes to bed at night, he
> *Snores, snores, snores.*   (DRAWN-OUT)

When he runs his shoes they go
> *Scruff, scruff, scruff.*   (ROUGHLY)

Jeremiah Obadiah,
> *Puff, puff, puff.*   (SLOWLY)

>   —*Author unknown.*

What Does the Weather Say?

What does the wind say?
> *"Whoooo, whoooo, whoooo."*   (HOWLING)

What does the hail say?
> *"Clatter, clatter, clatter."*   (NOISILY)

What does the rain say?
> *"Pitter-pat, pitter-pat, pitter-pat."*   (EVENLY)

What does the sleet say?
> *"Shush, shush, shush."*   (SOFT SLIDING SOUND)

What does the sun say?

What does the sun say?   (ASK LAST LINE VERY
                                              QUESTIONINGLY — THEN
                                              GENTLY PLACE FINGER
                                              ON LIP.)

>   —*Author unknown.*

Magic Lanterns

Fairy lanterns in the park
> *Twinkle! twinkle! twinkle!*
How they glimmer in the dark —
> *Twinkle! twinkle! twinkle!*
Fireflies make a merry light
Dancing, gleaming through the night,
Oh, they are a pretty sight.
> *Twinkle! twinkle! twinkle!*
>   — *Grace Rowe.* *

---

*Choral Speaking Arrangements for the Lower Grades, *by Louise Abney and Grace Rowe,* Expression Co., Mass., 1937, 1953.

Old Jack Frost

Who gives the tree its new fall suit?
    Old Jack Frost.
Who sweetens up the ripened fruit?
Who makes the birds fly a warmer route?
    Old Jack Frost.
Who brings the walnut tumbling down?
Who makes the chestnut sweet and brown?
Who yellows up the pumpkin's gown?
    Old Jack Frost.

Who makes the lace-designed windows?
    Old Jack Frost.
Who nips the tip of your chilly nose?
Who bites even at bundled-up toes?
    Old Jack Frost.
Who makes the white snow pile up deep?
Who makes you crawl up in a heap?
And call for covers when you sleep?
    Old Jack Frost.
                — Author unknown.

Snow Flakes

Feathery flakes of snow come down,
    Swirling, twirling, drifting,
Until they cover all the town,
    Swirling, twirling, drifting.

People hurry to and fro,
    Riding, sliding, skipping,
Through the silver-powdered snow,
    Riding, sliding, skipping.

Motor cars are going home,
    Shifting, swerving, dripping —
Through the swirling snowy-foam,
    Shifting, swerving, dripping.
                — Louise Abney. *

*Choral Speaking Arrangements for the Lower Grades.

Dem Bones Are Gonna...Rise Again

Old Noah and his wife, come one by one;
The Ark is a-ready for all to come.
    Dem bones, dem bones are gonna...rise again.

In come the animals two by two;
One is false and the other true.
    Dem bones, dem bones are gonna...rise again.

In come the animals three by three;
They're all set for a jamboree.
    Dem bones, dem bones are gonna...rise again.

In come the animals four by four;
Two through the window and two through the door.
    Dem bones, dem bones are gonna...rise again.

In come the animals five by five;
Almost dead and hardly alive.
    Dem bones, dem bones are gonna...rise again.

In come the animals six by six;
Three with clubs and three with sticks.
    Dem bones, dem bones are gonna...rise again.

In come the animals seven by seven;
Some from below and the others from heaven.
    Dem bones, dem bones are gonna...rise again.

In come the animals eight by eight;
Four on time and the other four late.
    Dem bones, dem bones are gonna...rise again.

In come the animals nine by nine;
Six in front and three behind.
    Dem bones, dem bones are gonna...rise again.

In come the animals ten by ten;
Went back out and come in again.
    Dem bones, dem bones are gonna...rise again.

All the animals come, and the flooded terrain;
The Ark is a-rising in the rain.

Dem bones, dem bones are gonna…rise again!
Dem bones are gonna rise again!
— *Traditional American chant.*

This is very effective with different individuals taking turns saying the verses, and the entire group chanting the refrain. In reciting the refrain, pause after saying *gonna*. Hold the word *rise* in a long ascending tone, then conclude with *again*.

One Misty Moisty Morning

One misty moisty morning,
    (Misty moisty morning.)
When cloudy was the weather.
I chanced to meet an old man,
Clothed all in leather.
    (Leather.)

He began to compliment,
And I began to grin,
    (In, in.)
With "How do you do," and "How do you do,"
And "How do you do again?"
    (And "How do you do again?")
        — *Mother Goose rhyme.*

The refrains are spoken like an echo.

The Easter Rabbit Is Coming

The Easter Rabbit is coming to town.
Will his fur be white or will it be brown?
    Hippety, hippety, hop.   (HAPPILY)

Carefully balanced on one of his legs,
He'll carry a basket of colored eggs.
    Hippety, hippety, hop.   (GENTLY, CAREFULLY)

He'll move around without any fuss,
While he hops upstairs to peek at us.
    Hippety, hippety, hop.   (ASCENDING TONES)

He'll make quite sure we're sleeping, then,
He'll quickly go back down again.
    Hippety, hippety, hop.   (DESCENDING TONES)

While we sleep he will quietly scurry,
To hide the Easter eggs in a hurry.
    Hippety, hippety, hop.   (VERY QUICKLY)

Some he'll hide upon the floor,
Low behind the kitchen door.
    Hippety, hippety, hop.   (LOW VOICE RANGE)

Perhaps we'll find one when we look,
High on a shelf behind a book.
    Hippety, hippety, hop.   (HIGH VOICE RANGE)

He'll hide the eggs around the house,
Moving quietly as a mouse.
    Hippety, hippety, hop.   (WHISPER)

When all the eggs are hidden, then,
He'll hop away from our house again.
    Hippety, hippety, hop.   (GAILY HOPPING)

When we wake up next morning, though,
We'll hunt for the eggs, and we will go...
    Hippety, hippety, hop.   (FAST AND LOUD)
                         — *Gloria T. Delamar.*

An Old Woman All Skin and Bone

There was an old woman all skin and bone,
She lived on a hillside all alone.
    O-o-o-o-o.

She'd go to church one day,
To hear the parson preach and pray.
    O-o-o-o-o.

When she got to the churchyard stile,
She thought she'd stop to rest a while.
    O-o-o-o-o.

When she got to the churchyard door,
She thought she'd stop to rest some more.
    O-o-o-o-o.

And when she got to the church within,
She thought she'd stop and rest again.
    O-o-o-o-o.

She looked up high and then looked down,
A ghastly corpse lay on the ground.
 O-o-o-o-o.

From eyes and mouth and ears and chin,
The worms crawled out and the worms crawled in.
 O-o-o-o-o.

The woman to the parson said,
Will I look so when I am dead?
 O-o-o-o-o.

The parson to the woman said,
Yes, you will look so when you are dead.
 O-o-o-o-o.

The old woman all skin and bone, then said,
 E-e-e-e-e!   (SCREAM)
       —Author unknown.

Let this get scarier and scarier as it goes on. The *Ooooo* should be like the oo's in *zoom*.

Christmas Bells Are Everywhere

Christmas bells are everywhere;
 Jingle jingle jhere.
The corner Santa rings his bell;
 Jingle jingle jell.
The bells upon the trolley clang;
 Jingle jingle jang.
Registers ring up the cash;
 Jingle jingle jash.
Ovens ring for baking cakes;
 Jingle jingle jakes.
Dinner bells give out their tinkle;
 Jingle jingle jinkle.
The bells worn on corsages ring;
 Jingle jingle jing.
Christmas trees have bells that tink;
 Jingle jingle jink.
Doorbells ring for many folks;
 Jingle jingle jolks.
Across the air the churches chime;
 Jingle jingle jime.

Christmas bells are all around,
With their merry Christmas sound.
They sing out and they ringle;
Jingle jingle jingle.
— *Gloria T. Delamar.*

Ho Ho Ho

It's time for Santa to be on his way,
With packs of toys upon his sleigh.
Ho ho ho!   (HAPPILY)
Up and up into the sky,
Over the housetops he will fly.
Ho ho ho!   (ASCENDING TONES)
Around and round the world he'll go,
Through the fluffy flakes of snow.
Ho ho ho!   (SOARING)
Then down he'll come upon the roofs,
While his reindeer prance their hoofs.
Ho ho ho!   (DESCENDING TONES)
Down the chimney he will come,
To fill the stockings full of fun.
Ho ho ho!   (MYSTERIOUSLY)
Dolls for girls and pretty rings,
Drums for boys and sporty things.
Ho ho ho!   (CONFIDING)
With a twinkle in his eyes,
Up the chimney he will rise.
Ho ho ho!   (QUICKLY RISING TONES)
Away he'll fly with calls of cheer,
And he won't be back for another year.
Ho ho ho!   (FULL AND SLOW)
— *Gloria T. Delamar.*

The Birds

From out of a wood did the cuckoo fly,
Cuckoo,
He came to a manager with joyful cry,
Cuckoo,
He hopped, he curtsied, round he flew,
And loud his jubilation grew,
Cuckoo, cuckoo, cuckoo.

A pigeon flew over to Galilee,
 Vrercroo,
He strutted, and cooed, and was full of glee,
 Vrercroo,
And showed with jewelled wings unfurled,
His joy that Christ was in the world,
 Vrercroo, vrercroo, vrercroo.

A dove settled down upon Nazareth,
 Tsucroo,
And tenderly chanted with all his breath,
 Tsucroo,
"O you," he cooed, "so good and true,
My beauty do I give to you —
 Tsucroo, tsucroo, tsucroo."
     — Czechoslovakian folk verse.

Bird calls are on different pitch levels: *Cuckoo* — first syllable moderate tone, second a few notes lower. *Vrercoo* — first syllable moderate tone, second a few notes higher. *Tsucroo* — both syllables high and soft on same note.

Long, Long Ago

Winds through the olive trees
Softly did blow,
Round little Bethlehem,
 Long, long ago.
Sheep on the hillside lay
Whiter than snow,
Shepherds were watching them,
 Long, long ago.
Then from the happy sky,
Angels bent low,
Singing their songs of joy,
 Long, long ago.
For in a manger bed,
Cradled we know,
A baby came to Bethlehem,
 Long, long ago.
     — Author unknown.

The Christmas Pudding

Into the basin put the plums,
   Stirabout, stirabout, stirabout!
Next the good white flour comes,
   Stirabout, stirabout, stirabout!
Sugar and peel and eggs and spice,
   Stirabout, stirabout, stirabout!
Mix them and fix them and cook them twice,
   Stirabout, stirabout, stirabout!
               —Author unknown.

I Saw Three Ships

I saw three ships come sailing in,
   On Christmas day, on Christmas day,
I saw three ships come sailing in,
   On Christmas day in the morning.

And what was in those ships all three?
   On Christmas day, on Christmas day.
And what was in those ships all three?
   On Christmas in the morning.

'Twas Jesus Christ and His Lady,
   On Christmas day, on Christmas day.
'Twas Jesus Christ and His Lady,
   On Christmas day in the morning.

Pray, whither sailed those ships all three?
   On Christmas day, on Christmas day.
Pray, whither sailed those ships all three?
   On Christmas day in the morning.

O, they sailed into Bethlehem,
   On Christmas day, on Christmas day.
O' they sailed into Bethlehem,
   On Christmas day in the morning.

And all the bells on earth shall ring,
   On Christmas day, on Christmas day.
And all the bells on earth shall ring,
   On Christmas day in the morning.

And all the angels in heaven shall sing,
  On Christmas day, on Christmas day.
And all the angels in heaven shall sing,
  On Christmas day in the morning.

And all the souls on earth shall sing,
  On Christmas day, on Christmas day.
And all the souls on earth shall sing,
  On Christmas day in the morning.

Then let us all rejoice again,
  On Christmas day, on Christmas day.
Then let us all rejoice again,
  On Christmas day in the morning.
                    — Old English carol.

6. Counting-Out Rhymes

These rhymes are used as a means of "choosing." Individuals can be chosen to be "it." The "it" may be chosen to take a certain role in a game or perform a certain privilege or task. Groups can be divided into teams by means of "counting out." Each alternate "it" can be assigned to a different team. These rhymes serve as a way of avoiding favoritism, in situations where someone must be chosen from a group. The saying and counting out of these rhymes is a game in itself, which everyone can enjoy.

Ways to Use Counting-Out Rhymes

The counting-out rhyme to choose who will be "it" may be recited by someone who will not be playing, or by one of the group. An "it" who is one of the group, includes him or herself in the counting out. Each count can be on the word, on the rhythmical stress (most common) or in some cases on the syllable.

1. *People*: Point to each person in turn while saying the rhyme. The person who is being pointed to when the final word is said is "it."

2. *Two fists*: Have everyone hold out both fists. Count out fists. When a fist is counted out, the player puts it behind his back. The first person to have both fists counted out is "it."

3. *The fingers*: Have everyone hold out both hands, with fingers spread wide. Count out fingers. As each finger is counted out, it is folded down into the hand. The first person to have all ten fingers counted out is "it."

4. *Last left*: To make a longer game of the counting out, or to add more suspense (especially if the "it" is to get to do something special), continue saying the rhyme until there is only one person left. He will then be "it." This can be done by counting out People, Two Fists or Ten Fingers. Rhymes which end with the word *out* are particularly suited to Last Left. The person reciting might want to say the same rhyme over and over, or may decide to use more than one counting-out rhyme.

Note that the following rhymes have no particular titles nor any identifiable authors.

114

EENIE, MEENIE, minie, mo,
Catch a monkey by the toe.
If he hollers, let him go,
Eenie, meenie, minie, mo.
And out goes Y-O-*U*.

OCKA, BOCKA, soda crocka,
Ocka, bocka, boo.
In comes Uncle Sam,
And out goes Y-O-*U*.

ME, MYSELF, and I,
Went to the kitchen and ate a pie.
Then my mother, she came in,
And chased us out with a rolling pin.
And this is the one she *caught*.

LITTLE PIGS at the table,
Ought to eat in the stable.
You can stay if you're able,
But you go *out*.

HACKAMORE, hickamore,
Packamore, pickamore,
Hack, hick, pack, *pick*.

CAPTAIN over the ocean,
Sailor over the sea.
The compass comes around to point,
And it points at *thee*.

INTERY, MINTERY, cutery, corn,
Apple seed and apple thorn,
O-U-T spells *out*.

INTERY, MINTERY, country corn,
Apple seed and apple thorn.
Wire briar, limber lock,
How many geese were in the flock?
Some flew east and some flew west,
And one flew over the cuckoo's nest.
O-N-E spells one is *it*.

ONE, TWO, three,
Says out goes *he* (or *she*).

A PENNY ON the avenue,
Two pennies on the sea,
Three pennies on the railroad,
And out goes *he* (or *she*).

COLUMBUS crossed the ocean blue,
In fourteen-hundred and ninety-two.
Three ships came sailing with him, too,
Just to say the "it" is *you*.

EENIE, MEENIE, dixie, deenie,
Hit 'em a lick, dee-King, dee-Queenie.
Round about,
Down and *out*.

ONE, TWO, three, four, five, six, seven,
All good children go to heaven,
When they get there, they will shout,
O-U-T, and that means *out*.

BIG BIT, little bit,
Have a fit,
You are *it*.

HI-CHEE, KI-CHEE, domin-i-chee,
Deel-ya, dal-ya, spit.
Hi-chee, ki-chee, domin-i-chee,
You are *it*.

PADDY-WACKY, Captain Dan,
Paddlewheeler, steamboat man.
Up the river, down the river,
Out goes *you*.

YOU CAN stand,
Or you can sit.
But if you play,
You must be *it*.

YOU CAN stay,
Or you can quit.
But if you're in,
You must be *it*.

IBBETY, Bobbety, boo,
Y-O-U spells *you*.

FIND A WITCH and find a fairy,
Find it in the dictionary,
I-T spells *it*.

CHICK, CHICK, chatterman,
How much are your geese?
Chick, chick, chatterman,
Fifty cents apiece.
Chick, chick, chatterman,
That's too dear,
Chick, chick, chatterman,
You get out of *here*.

ICKY, BICKY, soda cricky,
Icky, bicky, boo.
Icky, bicky, here's the tricky
Out goes *you*.

ONE POTATO, two potatoes,
Three potatoes, four,
Five potatoes, six potatoes,
Seven potatoes, more.
Hot potato! *You*.

ONE, TWO, three O'Leary,
Four, five, six O'Leary,
Seven, eight, nine O'Leary,
Ten O'Leary, then,
You are *it*.

HICKORY, DICKORY, dock,
The mouse ran up the clock.
The clock struck one,
The mouse ran down.
Hickory, dickory, dock-a-chime,
You're the one who's it this *time*.

ALL THE CATS consulted;
What was it about?
How to catch a little mouse,
Running in and *out*.

THE BUS will soon
Come into view,
And then it will stop
Here for *you*.

ENGINE, ENGINE, number nine,
Running on the Chicago line.
Engine, engine, number nine,
When she's polished, she will shine.
And stop for *you*.

GIVE THREE cheers
For the red, white and blue.
One, two, three,
And out goes *you*.

FUDGE, FUDGE, tell the judge,
Sister made some candy.
Here us shout,
Throw it *out*.

STEP OVER land,
Step over sea,
Step aside,
For out goes *he* (or *she*).

EENIE, MEENIE, tipsie, teenie,
Jumping Jack and Josephinie,
My mother said to pick
This *one*.

SPANISH DANCER, do the splits,
Spanish dancer, do high kicks.
Spanish dancer, clicks a shoe,
Spanish dancer, chooses *you*.

IT'S RAINING, it's pouring,
The old man's snoring;
And that means
You are *it*.

ANNADY, MANNADY, mickady, me,
Abbady, babbady, bump-a-knee.
Over, under, in, *out*.

SEE-SAW, sacradown,
Which is the way to London-town?
One foot up, the other foot down,
That is the way to London-town.
Down. Town. *Down*.

HOT-CROSS BUNS, hot-cross buns,
One a penny, two a penny,
Hot-cross buns.
Who ate a bun?
You are the *one*.

ONE, TWO, three, four,
Mary at the cottage door,
Five, six, seven, eight,
Eating cherries off a plate.
O-U-T spells *out*.

ONE, TWO, three, four, five,
I caught a hare alive,
Six, seven, eight, nine, ten,
I let him go again.
O-U-T spells *out*.

MEENA, DEENA, deena, duss.
Catala, weena, weena, wuss.
Spit, spot, must be done,
Twiddlum, twaddlum, twenty-one.
You're the *one*.

INTY, MINTY, tibbety fig,
Deemy, dimey, doma nig,
Howchy, powchy, doma nowchy,
Out goes *you*.

HICKORY, DICKORY, six and seven,
Alabone, crackabone, ten, eleven,
Spin, spun, muskadit,
Ninety-nine, you are *it*.

IBBETY, BIBBETY, gibbety goat,
Ibbety, bibbety, bobbety boat,
Dictionary,
Down the ferry,
Out goes *you*.

OVER THE LAKE, over the sea,
Over the ocean blue.
Up the river, down the river,
Out goes *you*.

SAY YOU'RE healthy,
Say you're sick,
This is the one,
I will *pick*.

ICKY, BICKY, cricky, tricky,
Icky, bicky, boo.
Icky, bicky, cricky, tricky,
Out goes *you*.

ROSES ARE red,
Violets are blue,
Sugar is sweet,
And so are *you*.

I ASKED my mother what I should do
My mother said I should pick *you*.

AS I CLIMBED up the apple tree,
All the apples fell on me.
Someone shook them, and I knew,
The one who did, was Y-O-*U*.

I SCREAM, you scream,
We all scream for ice cream.
Who screams loudest?
Y-O-*U*.

SMARTY, SMARTY, had a party,
Nobody there but smarty, smarty.
Smarty, smarty, threw a fit,
Smarty, smarty, you are *it*.

BLUE BELLS, cockle shells,
Eevy, ivy, over.
My mother said to choose
This *one*.

IN AND UNDER, round about,
Teacher said O-U-T spells *out*.

ONE, TWO, three, four, five, six, seven,
All good children go to heaven.
But not *you*.

OPEN YOUR mouth and close your eyes,
And I'll give you something to make you wise.
Y-O-U are *out*.

ICE CREAM, candy, apple pie,
Did you ever tell a lie?
If you did, holler *I*.

MONKEY, MONKEY, in a tree,
How many monkeys will there be?
One, two, three,
Out goes *he* (or *she*).

MY MOTHER, your mother,
Live across the way,
Every night, they have a fight,
And this is what they say;
Ocka, bocka, soda, crocka,
Ocka, bocka, boo.
Your old man chews tobacco,
And so do *you*.

A, B, C, d, e, f, g, h, i, j, k, l, m, n, o, p, q,
    r, s, t, u are *out* (or *it*).

SAY THE VOWELS in the alphabet,
A, e, i, o, u are *it*.

ROSES ARE red,
Violets are blue,
When I choose
It will be *you*.

IN AND OUT, in and out,
Around the circle all about,
When we know, we will shout,
You are in and you are *out*.

EEVY, IVY, eevy, ivy, eevy, ivy over.
Professor Bright, a learn-ed man,
Teaches children all he can.
First to read, and then to write,
Eevy, ivy, you are *out*.

MY POP, your pop,
Live across the street,

Thirty-nine-twenty-six
Pennsylvania street.
Every night, they have a fight,
And this is what they say;
Inky dinky, feet so stinky,
Dip them in the muddy drinky.
Hear them shout.
You are *out*.

EERY, IRY, ickery, am,
Hare-um, scare-um, bare-um,
Tic, tac, toe, 'tis *you*.

COWBOY, COWBOY, driving cattle,
Can you hear his silver rattle?
One, two, three,
Out goes *he* (or *she*).

MONKEY IN the jailhouse,
Don't you hear him holler?
Took a pickle from a fish
And didn't pay a dollar.
One, two, three,
Out goes *he* (or *she*).

A MONKEY washed a window,
With a cup of cocoa,
The window broke,
The monk got soaked.
Monkey, dunkey, out-*O*.

Double-It Counting-Out Rhymes

These particular counting-out rhymes have two underlined words.
The first underlined word indicates the "it" who will determine how the
rest of the rhyme will be played out. From there, the word indicated is
spelled out, or the number counted off, until the final "it" is reached.
(With almost all of these, the word "out" may be used instead of "it," if
desired.)

Be you dark or be you fair,
What is the color of your *hair*? (brown, black, yellow, red)
R-E-D, and you are *it* (or *out*).

Count your fingers, count your thumbs,
Tell me when your birthday *comes*. (person names
   birth month)
      M-A-Y, and you are *it*.

My Mom and your Mom were hanging out clothes,
My Mom hit your Mom right on the nose.
What color was the *blood*? (person names a color)
      G-R-E-E-N, and you are *it*.

Bubblegum, bubblegum, in a dish,
How many pieces do you *wish*? (person chooses a
   number from 1 to 10)
      F-I-V-E, and you are *it*.

Here's your fortune, here's your fame,
Now's the time to say your *name*. (person states name
   or nickname)
      W-I-L-L-I-A-M, and you are *it*.

Starting Chants for Races

Ready? Get set! Go!

One, two, three, go!

On your mark! Get set! Go!

One for the money, two for the show, three to get ready,
   and four to *go*.

Red, white, blue, one, two, three, skidoo!

7. Jump-Rope and Bounce-Ball Chants

Counting chants can be effectively used for jump-rope, bounce-ball, paddle-ball, one-legged hopping, etc. These chants serve as an amusing way to encourage the practice of certain activities and to score one's ability at performing the action. In addition, the number and alphabet chants enforce the learning of numbers and the alphabet by younger children. Older children enjoy the "answer" which is obtained from their "counted-off" performance.

Ways to Use Chants

The number and alphabet-counting chants in this chapter can be used for jump-rope, bounce-ball, paddle-ball, and one-legged hopping. When using the number-counting chants, it is sometimes a good idea to limit the number of times a player may jump. Of course, if players are trying to "set a record" then no limit would be put on them!

When using the alphabet-counting chants, the players get an "answer" when they "miss" the bounce of the ball or the jump over the rope. One can also decide to "miss on purpose" to pick a certain letter of the alphabet!

Further back in this chapter are some chants just for bounce-ball and some chants just for jump-rope. There are also some pages that give different ways to jump-rope and different ways to turn the rope.

> WIRE, BRIAR, limberlock,
> Three geese in a flock.
> One flew east, and one flew west,
> And one flew over the cuckoo's nest.
> How many eggs were in the nest?
> 1, 2, 3, etc.

I HATE to wash the dishes,
I hate to scrub the floor.
I'd rather kiss my sweetheart,
Behind the kitchen door.
How many kisses will I get?
1, 2, 3, etc.

BOBBY SHAFTO, climb a tree,
Bobby Shafto, scrape your knee.
Bobby Shafto, toss a kiss,
Bobby Shafto, never miss.
How many kisses, will he toss?
1, 2, 3, etc.

LITTLE GEORGIE Washington,
Never told a lie.
Went into the kitchen,
And ate a cherry pie.
How many cherries were in the pie?
1, 2, 3, etc.

ABRAHAM-A Lincoln, never was a crook.
Because his nose, was always in a book.
How many books did he read?
1, 2, 3, etc.

HERE COMES the teacher with a big fat stick,
Now get ready for arithmetic.
1, 2, 3, etc.

MOTHER, MOTHER, I feel sick,
Call the doctor, quick, quick, quick.
Doctor, Doctor, will I die?
Yes, my dear, and so shall I.
How many carriages will there be?
1, 2, 3, etc.

MAGGIE, MAGGIE, where is Jiggs?
Down in the cellar, eating pigs.
How many pigs will he eat?
1, 2, 3, etc.

I LIKE TO JUMP, I like to bump,
If I fall I'll get a lump.
How many lumps will I get?
1, 2, 3, etc.

MY MOTHER owns a butcher shop,
My father cuts the meat,
And I am just their little kid,
Who runs across the street.
How many times do I cross?
1, 2, 3, etc.

BREAD AND butter, sugar and spice.
How many boys (girls), think I'm nice?
1, 2, 3, etc.

LAST NIGHT, the night before,
A lemon and a pickle
Came knocking at my door.
I opened the door, to let them in,
And they hit me on the head
With a rolling-pin.
How many times
Did they hit me on the head?
1, 2, 3, etc.

BLUEBELLS, cockleshells,
Eevy, ivy, over.
Tell your mother to hold her tongue,
She had a boy when she was young.
Tell your father to do the same,
He had a girl and he changed her name.
How many sweethearts did they have?
1, 2, 3, etc.

I LIKE COFFEE, I like tea.
How many boys (girls) are crazy for me?
1, 2, 3, etc.

OLD MAN Daisy, he went crazy.
Up the ladder, down the ladder,
1, 2, 3, etc.

MY BROTHER (sister) broke a bottle,
And blamed it all on me.
I told Ma,
She told Pa.
Brother (sister) got a spanking.
Ha, ha, ha.
How many spanks did he (she) get?
1, 2, 3, etc.

DOWN IN the meadow where the green grass grows,
There sat (girl's name) as pretty as a rose.
She sang, she sang,
She sang so sweet.
Along came her sweetheart (or say a boy's name),
And kissed her on the cheek.
How many kisses did he give her in a week?
1, 2, 3, etc.

DOWN IN the valley where the green grass grows,
There sat (boy's name) in his old clothes.
He put his bare feet
Into the creek,
When along came his sweetheart (or say a girl's name),
And kissed him on the cheek.
How many kisses did she give him in a week?
1, 2, 3, etc.

CINDERELLA, dressed in yellow,
Went downtown to meet her fellow.
How many kisses did she get?
1, 2, 3, etc.

TIM, TIM, sat on a pin.
How many inches did it go in?
1, 2, 3, etc.

GRACE, GRACE, dressed in lace,
In front of the mirror, powdering her face.
How much powder did she use?
1, 2, 3, etc.

FUDGE, FUDGE, tell the judge,
Mamma's got a new-born baby.
Wrap it up in tissue paper,
Send it up the elevator.
How many floors will it ride?
1, 2, 3, etc.

DOCTOR, DOCTOR, tell me quick,
How many days will I be sick?
1, 2, 3, etc.

DOCTOR, DOCTOR, tell no lie,
How many years before I die?
1, 2, 3, etc.

WHEN YOU'RE married, open up a can,
And dump it on a dish for your old man.
And then count your children, if you can.
1, 2, 3, etc.

PEASE PORRIDGE hot, pease porridge cold.
Pease porridge in a pot, full of mold,
How many days has it been in the pot?
1, 2, 3, etc.

POSTMAN, POSTMAN, do your duty.
Mail this letter to my cutie.
Postman, postman, don't delay,
Send it to him (her) right away.
How many days will the letter take?
1, 2, 3, etc.

SAILOR, SAILOR, over the sea,
All he could see, was sea, sea, sea.
How many days was he sea-sick?
1, 2, 3, etc.

TILLIE THE TOILER, sat on a boiler,
The boiler got hot, Tillie got shot.
How many times did Tillie get shot?
1, 2, 3, etc.

MABEL, MABEL, set the table,
Company's coming for dinner.
How many people will there be?
1, 2, 3, etc.

BILLY GAVE me apples,
Billy gave me pears.
Billy gave me fifty cents,
And kissed me on the stairs.
I gave him back his apples,
I gave him back his pears.
I gave him back his fifty cents,
And kicked him down the stairs.
How many stairs did he roll down?
1, 2, 3, etc.

SITTING ON the garden gate,
Eating raisins off a plate.
How many raisins did I eat?
1, 2, 3, etc.

MONKEY, MONKEY, bottle of beer,
How many monkeys have we here?
1, 2, 3, etc.

ONE, TWO, three, four, five,
I caught a mackeral-fish alive.
Six, seven, eight, nine, ten,
I threw the fish back in again.
How many times did I do that?
1, 2, 3, etc.

MY MOTHER is a dancer,
Oh, how she can twist!
She can do the hootchy-kootchy,
Just like this.
1, 2, 3, etc.

SITTING ON the railroad, picking up stones.
Along came an engine, and broke my bones.
"Oh," I said, "that's not fair."
"Oh," said the engineer, "I don't care."
How many bones did I break?
1, 2, 3, etc.

I WENT DOWN to Grandpa's farm,
Billygoat chased me round the barn.
Chased me up the apple tree,
Butted the tree to get at me.
How many apples, ripe and red,
Fell on that old billygoat's head?
1, 2, 3, etc.

MA AND PA went to town,
Mama bought an evening gown.
Papa bought a pair of shoes,
Then he bought the Daily News.
How many pages did he read?
1, 2, 3, etc.

I WAS TAKING a wee little piggy,
Down to the animal fair,
He grew into a big fat hog,
Before he ever got there.
How many pounds did he weigh?
1, 2, 3, etc.

I EAT MY peas with honey,
I've done it all my life.
It makes the peas taste funny,
But it keeps them on my knife.
How many peas can I get on a knife?
1, 2, 3, etc.

HELLO, HELLO, hello, sir,
Tell me where you were, sir.
   Fishing in the creek, sir,
   I go there every week, sir.
Did you catch some fish, sir?
   Yes, I caught a batch, sir.
How many did you catch, sir?
   One, sir, two, sir, three, sir, etc.

ONE FOR the money,
Two for the show,
Three to get ready,
To count as I go.
1, 2, 3, etc.

LADYBUG, LADYBUG, fly away home,
Your house is on fire,
And your children will burn.
How many children will burn down?
1, 2, 3, etc.

I CAN DO a polka, I can do a split,
I can do a tap dance, just like this,
1, 2, 3, etc.

I'M THE WITCH of Rotterdam,
Can you guess how old I am?
1, 2, 3, etc.

ICE CREAM, candy, cake and butter.
What's the name of my true lover?
A, B, C, etc.

When letter is determined, player must give a name starting with that letter.

BLUEBERRY, raspberry, strawberry jam,
What are the initials of my young man?
A, B, C, etc.

TEACHER nearly had a fit,
When I learned the alphabet.
Seems I wasn't very bright,
I could never get it right.
I always got stuck after —
A, B, C, etc.

WHAT SHALL I name my little pup?
I'll have to think a good one up.
A, B, C, etc.

When letter is determined, player names something beginning with it.

IF I COULD change my name-us,
I would soon be famous.
What would I change it to?
A, B, C, etc.

When letter is determined, player names something beginning with it.

STRAWBERRY shortcake, huckleberry jam,
Tell me the initials of your old man.
A, B, C, etc.

HERE I GO, here I go,
Tell me the initials of my best beau.
A, B, C, etc.

SWEET AND sour pickles,
Sugar, cake and cream.
Tell the initials of my dream.
A, B, C, etc.

When letter is determined, player names something dreamt about.

SHAME ON ME, shame, shame, shame.
I've got a secret lover,
Don't even know his (her) name.
Jump to find it, jump!
A, B, C, etc.

A, B, C's, and vegetable goop,
What will I find in the alphabet soup?
A, B, C, etc.

When letter is determined, player names something found in the soup.

Some Chants Just for Bounce-Ball

BOUNCY, BOUNCY, ball-y,
I broke the head off my dolly,
My Mom came out,
And gave me a clout,
That turned my petticoat
Inside out.　　　　　　　　　(TURN LEG OVER BALL)

RIGHT HAND beats a booming drum,　(BOUNCE BALL WITH RIGHT HAND)
Left hand beats a pan.　　　　　　(BOUNCE BALL WITH LEFT HAND)
But I can bounce my ball-o,　　　　(ALTERNATE RIGHT AND LEFT
Using either hand.　　　　　　　　HAND TO BOUNCE BALL)

GYPSY, GYPSY, lived in a tent.
Gypsy couldn't pay her rent.
She borrowed one, she borrowed two,
And passed the ball to Y-O-U.　　(AT Y, PASS BALL TO A PLAYER)

Bounce the ball while saying the following verses, turning leg over the ball when verse says to do so, and also performing actions suitable to words like "eat a bun."

1. One, one, eat a bun, right foot over, one, one, one.
   Two, two, touch your shoe, right foot over, two, two, two.
   Three, three, bend a knee, right foot over, three, three, three.
   Four, four, touch the floor, right foot over, four, four, four.
   Five, five, reach for the sky, right foot over, five, five, five.
   Six, six, pick up sticks, right foot over, six, six, six.
   Seven, seven, look to heaven, right foot over, seven, seven, seven.
   Eight, eight, shut the gate, right foot over, eight, eight, eight.
   Nine, nine, draw a line, right foot over, nine, nine, nine.
   Ten, ten, this is the end, right foot over, ten, ten, ten.

2. Repeat entire verse — saying left foot over.

3. Repeat entire verse — at odd numbers say right foot (1, 3, 5, 7, 9);
   at even numbers say left foot (2, 4, 6, 8, 10).

The Barney-Boy Bounce

In this game, a leg is turned over the ball every time the word *over* is spoken. After players can perform this easily, they can add motions to suit the words every time they say the second line. Here is a tip about turning a leg over the ball; if the ball is being bounced with the right hand, it is easiest to turn the leg over the ball from left to right. More experienced players may want to try this routine using a ball about the size of a tennis ball. This will be even harder to do when the actions are added.

When Barney-boy was one,
He learned to suck his thumb.
Over Barney, over Barney,
Half past one.

When Barney-boy was two,
He learned to tie his shoe,
Over Barney, over Barney,
Half past two.

When Barney-boy was three,
He always touched his knee,
Over Barney, over Barney,
Half past three.

When Barney-boy was four,
He always touched the floor,
Over Barney, over Barney,
Half past four.

When Barney-boy was five,
He learned to wink his eye,
Over Barney, over Barney,
Half past five.

When Barney-boy was six,
He helped to pick up sticks,
Over Barney, over Barney,
Half past six.

When Barney-boy was seven,
He watched the stars in heaven,
Over Barney, over Barney,
Half past seven.

When Barney-boy was eight,
He always shut the gate,
Over Barney, over Barney,
Half past eight.

When Barney-boy was nine,
He had a porcupine,
Over Barney, over Barney,
Half past nine.

When Barney-boy was ten,
His pet it was a hen,
Over Barney, over Barney,
Half past ten.

When Barney-boy was eleven,
He took a trip to Devon,
Over Barney, over Barney,
Half past eleven.

When Barney-boy was twelve,
He learned to make a shelf,
Over Barney, over Barney,
Half past twelve.

When Barney-boy was grown,
He sat on a throne,
Over Barney, over Barney,
Over Barney-boy.

Some players like to turn a leg over the ball every time they say the word *sir*, in the following chant.

Hello, hello, hello, sir,
Will you come out with me, sir?
No, sir.

Why, sir?
Because I have a cold, sir.
Let me hear you sneeze, sir.
Kerchoo, kerchoo, kerchoo, sir.

A Carload of Alphabets

In this ball-bouncing chant, the players are supposed to turn a leg over the ball each time they say one of the words which begins with the particular letter they are doing at the time. Any other names, places, or things can be substituted for the ones shown here. Boys can say "A — my name is Alex, my wife's name is Amy," and so on.

A — my name is Amy,
My husband's name is Albert,
And we came from Africa,
With a carload full of antelopes.

B — my name is Barbara,
My husband's name is Benjamin,
And we came from Buffalo,
With a carload full of bananas.

C — my name is Carol,
My husband's name is Christopher.
And we came from Canada,
With a carload full of cats.

D — my name is Daisy,
My husband's name is David,
And we came from Denmark,
With a carload full of diapers.

E — my name is Esther,
My husband's name is Ed,
And we came from Ethiopia,
With a carload full of eggs.

F — my name is Fanny,
My husband's name is Fred,
And we came from France,
With a carload full of Frenchmen.

G — my name is Gloria,
My husband's name is Glenn,
And we came from Georgia,
With a carload full of garbage.

H — my name is Hildegard,
My husband's name is Harry,
And we came from Honolulu,
With a carload full of honey.

I — my name is Isabel,
My husband's name is Isaac,
And we came from Iceland,
With a carload full of ice-cream.

J — my name is Joy,
My husband's name is Jeffrey,
And we came from Jerusalem,
With a carload full of jelly-beans,

K — my name is Katie,
My husband's name is Kenneth,
And we came from Kansas,
With a carload full of kangaroos.

L — my name is Laura,
My husband's name is Leo,
And we came from Los Angeles,
With a carload full of lampshades.

M — my name is Melinda,
My husband's name is Mark,
And we came from Maryland,
With a carload full of maps.

N — my name is Nancy,
My husband's name is Nick,
And we came from New York,
With a carload full of nuts.

O — my name is Olga,
My husband's name is Oliver,
And we came from Oshkosh,
With a carload full of owls.

P — my name is Polly,
My husband's name is Paul,
And we came from Pennsylvania,
With a carload full of pencils.

Q — my name is Queenie,
My husband's name is Quincy,
And we came from Quebec,
With a carload full of quartz.

R — my name is Rebecca,
My husband's name is Richard,
And we came from Russia,
With a carload full of rootbeer.

S — my name is Shirley,
My husband's name is Sam,
And we came from Switzerland,
With a carload full of socks.

T — my name is Tonie,
My husband's name is Thomas,
And we came from Timbuctoo,
With a carload full of toadstools.

U — my name is Ursula,
My husband's name is Utley,
And we came from Utah,
With a carload full of unicorns.

V — my name is Verda,
My husband's name is Vince,
And we came from Virginia,
With a carload full of violins.

W — my name is Wendy,
My husband's name is William,
And we came from Washington,
With a carload full of worms.

X — my name is Xenia,
My husband's name is Xander,
And we came from Xanthus,
With a carload full of xylophones.

Y — my name is Yvonne,
My husband's name is Yorick,
And we came from Yellowstone Park,
With a carload full of yaks.

Z — my name is Zelda,
My husband's name is Zeke,
And we came from the Zoo,
With a carload full of zithers.

The Triple-Bounce

This is a ball-bouncing game for two or more people to play. Two people can stand across from each other, but three or more players should form a circle. The players should stand just far enough apart to bounce the ball on the ground one time when it is passed to the player on the left.

The first player starts off by naming a subject. He or she should say it three times while bouncing the ball three times. Then the ball is bounced over to the player on the left.

The second player must then name a specific thing that belongs in that subject or category. He or she should say it three times while bouncing the ball three times. Then the ball is bounced over to the player on the left.

The next person can either name another specific thing that belongs to the same subject, or can call out another subject. He or she should say it three times while bouncing the ball three times. Then the ball is bounced over to the player on the left.

Everyone will have to listen carefully so as not to be caught off-guard. Players are allowed to repeat a subject used before, but they cannot repeat a specific thing that was used, unless a different subject has been done in between.

Here is how one game with five players might go:

Player number 1: Names of animals, names of animals, names of animals.
            2: Dogs, dogs, dogs.
            3: Pigs, pigs, pigs.
            4: Zebras, zebras, zebras.
            5: Names of cars, names of cars, names of cars.
            1: Ford, Ford, Ford.
            2: Names of flowers, names of flowers, names of flowers.
            3: Daisies, daisies, daisies.
            4: Tulips, tulips, tulips.
            5: Names of states, names of states, names of states.
            1: Pennsylvania, etc.

There are many different subjects which can be named. And every one of the subjects has lots of specific things to name. Here are some ideas for subjects:

animals	spices
cars	nuts
flowers	musical instruments
cities	birds
states	trees
streets	months
teachers	movie stars
presidents	singers
countries	furniture
vegetables	etc.
fruits	

Chants Just for Jump-Rope

ROOM for rent, inquire within,
When I run out, let (call out a name of another player)
     move in.

APARTMENT for rent, inquire within,
When A moves out, let B move in.
Apartment for rent, inquire within,
When B moves out, let C move in.
Apartment for rent, inquire within,
When C moves out, let D move in.
   And so on through the alphabet.

KEEP THE ROPE a-turning,
Just for (call name of a player),
And-a one, and-a two,
And-a one, two, three.

On *three*, first player runs out and one whose name was called runs in.

IF YOU'RE ABLE, set the table.
Don't forget the *salt*.
If you're able, set the table,
Don't forget the *pepper*.
If you're able, set the table,
Don't forget the *salt*, etc.

Turn rope slowly for *salt*, until word changes to *pepper*. Turn rope very fast for *pepper*, until word changes to *salt*. Continue alternating *salt* and *pepper* until player misses, or runs out.

JUMP-ROPE, jump-rope,
Will I miss?
Jump-rope, jump-rope Just watch *this*.

At *this*, player stops rope by stepping on it or by catching it.

MISS, MISS, little Miss, miss,
When she misses, she misses like *this*.

At *this*, player stops rope by stepping on it or by catching it.

JUMP AND MISS, jump and miss,
When I jump-rope, I miss like *this*.

At *this*, player stops rope by stepping on it or by catching it.

CAKE AND ice cream,
Pudding and pie.
You like them all
And so do I.

IF WE GOBBLE all the ick,
Will we both get very sick?
Yes, no, maybe so, etc.

BLUE, AND GREEN, and red, and yellow,
Has your sweetheart got another fellow?
Yes, no, maybe so, etc.

BLUE, AND GREEN, and red, and yellow,
Will I ever catch a fellow?
Yes, no, maybe so, etc.

I WENT DOWNTOWN, to see Miss Brown.
She gave me a nickel, to buy a pickle.
The pickle was sour, she gave me a flower.
The flower was dead, she gave me some thread.
The thread was black, she gave me a tack.
The tack was sharp, she gave me a harp.
The harp was broke, she gave me a cloak.
The cloak was tight, she gave me a kite.
The kite away flew, and I did *too*!

(PLAYER RUNS OUT AT *TOO*)

TEDDY BEAR, Teddy Bear, turn around,
Teddy Bear, Teddy Bear, touch the ground.

Teddy Bear, Teddy Bear, read the news,
Teddy Bear, Teddy Bear, click your shoes.

Teddy Bear, Teddy Bear, clap your hand,
Teddy Bear, Teddy Bear, touch the sand.

Teddy Bear, Teddy Bear, tie your shoe,
Teddy Bear, Teddy Bear, twenty-three *skidoo*.

Suit action to words with each line, while continuing to jump. Player
runs out on *skidoo*.

LAST NIGHT and the night before,
Three bold robbers came to my door.
When I went down to let them in,
They knocked me down with a rolling pin.
But I got up as quick as that,
And chased them away with a baseball bat.
One ran east, and one ran west,
And one jumped over the cuckoo's *nest*.

(PLAYER RUNS OUT ON *NEST*)

(NAME OF PLAYER) ate some marmalade,
(Name) drank some beer,
(Name) ate some other things,
(That made him (her) feel so queer.
    Oops went the marmalade,
    Oops went the beer,
    Oops went the other things,
    That made him (her) feel so queer.
        Oh, dear!   (PLAYER RUNS OUT ON 'DEAR')

(BOY'S NAME) and (Girl's name)
Sitting in a tree,
K-I-S-S-I-N-G,
First comes love,
And then comes marriage,
And then comes (name)
With a baby carriage.

The set of rhymes below can be used separately, or taken in order, to arrive at the answers.

    1. ICE CREAM SODA, ginger ale, pop,
       Tell me the name of my sweetheart.
           A, B, C, etc.

    2. DOES HE LOVE me? Tell me now.
           Yes, no, maybe so, etc.

    3. WHAT WILL my husband be?
       Rich man, poor man, beggarman, thief,
       Doctor, lawyer, merchant, chief, etc.

    4. WHAT WILL I be married in?
       Silk, satin, calico, rags, etc.

    5. WHAT WILL the stone in my ring be?
       Diamond, pebble, emerald, glass, etc.

    6. WHAT KIND of house will we live in?
       Little house, big house, mansion, barn, etc.

    7. HOW MANY CHILDREN will we have?
       1, 2, 3, etc.

ENGINE, ENGINE, number nine,
Coming down the Chicago line.
Hear it rumble, see it shine,
Engine, engine, number nine.

If the train should jump the track
Will I get my money back?
Yes, no, maybe so, etc.

RUNNING UP the escalator,
Riding down the elevator.
Up, down, when I die,
Will I go up or down?
Up, down, up, down, etc.

POLICEMAN, policeman, do your duty,
Here comes (name), The American Beauty. *
She likes salt,
But what she likes better,
Is plenty of that
red, hot, pepper!   (TURN ROPE VERY FAST)

*For a boy: "And he's no beauty."

I'M A LITTLE Dutch girl,
Dressed in blue.
Here are the things
I like to do.
Salute to the Captain,
Bow to the Queen,
And turn my back
On the ugly submarine.

MARCO POLO went to France
To show the ladies how to dance.
Heel and toe, curtsey now,
Marco Polo showed them how.

MARCO POLO went to France
To show the gentlemen how to dance.
First a kick, and then a bow,
Marco Polo showed them how.

I COUNTED up my pennies,
For to buy a ride.
What I'll get to ride on,
The pennies will decide.
Horse, truck, submarine, wagon, skates, limousine, etc.

HAD A LITTLE baby, dressed all bare.
Had a little baby, tossed it in the air.

Did it go up, did it go down?
Up, down, up, down, etc.

DUTCHMAN, DUTCHMAN, coming down the street,
Dutchman, Dutchman, hands upon his feet.
Dutchman, Dutchman, flying through the skies,
Dutchman, Dutchman, covered up his eyes.
Dutchman, Dutchman, sailing on a ship,
Dutchman, Dutchman, tongue upon his lip.
Dutchman, Dutchman, drank a jug of beer.
Dutchman, Dutchman, get out of *here*.

(AT *HERE* PLAYER RUNS OUT)

"I can jump-rope".....
    One!
"I can jump-rope".....
    Two!
"I can jump-rope".....
    Three!.....etc.

"I can jump-rope" is said while running into the rope. Person takes the appropriate number of jumps, then runs out.

I WENT TO the animal fair.
The birds and the beasts were there.
The big baboon by the light of the moon,
Was combing his auburn hair.
The monkey he got drunk,
And sat on the elephant's trunk.
The elephant sneezed, and fell on his knees,
And that was the end of the monkey-monk,
And that was the end of the monk.

A, B, C, one, two, three;
I want (call name of another player) to come in with me.

Person named runs in and jumps with first.

A, B, C, one, two, three;
I want (call name of another player) to come in with me.

Said by second jumper — thus a third person joins in.

A, B, C, one, two, three;
I want (name) to come in with me...etc.

Continue until all players are jumping together.

HAPPY HOOLIGAN, dressed so fine,
Hung his breeches on the line.
When the line began to swing,
Happy Hooligan began to sing.
"On the mountain stands a lady,
Who she is, I do not know.
All she wants is gold and silver,
And a young man for a beau."
Come in, come in (name of player outside rope)
Go out, go out (Name).

The first jumper says the verse first; after another jumper has been called in, that person says the verse next, and so on. On the last line, the name of the person who was in is spoken by the new person called in and the other player runs out.

Ways to Jump Rope

When jumping alone, players can jump any way they like. When jumping in groups, the jumper usually jumps until he or she misses or runs out at the end of a particular rhyme. Very good jumpers may want to agree on a certain number of jumps, such as 50, or 100, so that everyone will have time to get a turn. If it is a competition, though, no limit would be set on the number of jumps. The person jumping the longest would be the winner!

Salt: This is the basic way to jump rope. The rope is turned at a medium speed which allows the jumper to do a double-hop, one big hop and one little hop. Like this: HOP hop HOP hop, etc. or JUMP jump JUMP jump. This is done holding the feet fairly close together, but they do not have to touch each other.

Alternate Salt: First the right foot does the HOP hop, then the jumper shifts to the left foot to HOP hop, then back to the right foot again, and then again to the left, continuing to alternate feet.

One Foot Salt: The entire turn is done by jumping on one foot.

Pepper: The rope is turned very fast and the jumper must get over the rope with short, quick one-hops.

The Can-Can: Jump first on one foot, and then on the other, kicking out the alternate leg and knee each time in a "can-can" step.

Indian-Step: First with one foot, and then with the other, step over the rope each time alternately, without taking a little jump between each step. This is like taking giant steps in place while turning the rope slowly.

Spread-Eagle: Jump with the feet spread wide apart. This can be done either with or without the extra little hop.

Buck and Wing: Click heels together between jumps.

Clicks: Click the handles of the rope together between jumps.

Ways to Turn the Rope

Loners: One person, jumping alone, can turn the rope either forward or backward, or fast or slow, just as he or she wishes.

Up the Stairs: In general, the rope should just brush the ground as it comes around. To make it more difficult, the rope can be raised several inches from the ground (up the stairs).

Starting in Place: The jumper can stand beside the rope before the turners begin to turn it. The jumper must then start jumping when the rope comes around.

Running In: The jumper runs into the turning rope to take his or her place to jump.

Running into the Wall: The rope is turned toward the jumper. That is, when the rope is up overhead it will be heading toward the jumper.

Jumping over the Moon: The rope is turned away from the jumper. That is, when the rope is up overhead it will be heading away from the jumper.

Double Dutch: For more experienced jumpers, two ropes can be used. The turners spread their hands far apart and first start turning one rope, and then the other, so that the ropes touch the floor alternately. The ropes can both be turned inward, or they can both be turned outward.

Stars Overhead: To the first turn of the verse, the jumper jumps the regular way. Then as the last word of the verse is said, the player quickly stoops, and the turners raise the rope overhead and continue to turn it while the verse is being recited. As the last word of the verse is repeated, the jumper quickly jumps up and the turners move the rope back down into the usual position. The verse can be repeated alternately this way until the jumper misses or it has been performed an agreed number of times.

Other Rope Games

High Water, Low Water: Everyone lines up to jump over the rope, which is held taut, about five inches from the floor. As each player takes a turn, they run behind the turners and form into line again. When everyone has had a chance to jump over the water, the rope is raised another five inches, and everyone jumps over again. The rope is raised more each time, until there is only one person left who has not tripped up.

Over the Waves: This is similar to "high water, low water," except that the rope is wiggled back and forth so that it forms "waves" to jump over.

Through the Tunnel: The players line up and take turns running through the turning rope without being hit by the rope and without making any jumps. The rope can be turned toward the players (running into the wall) or away from the players (jumping over the moon).

The Swinging Cradle: The rope is swung back and forth without being turned over, like a cradle swinging. The players must jump back and forth over the rope until they miss. The rope can be slowly raised higher and higher to make the jumping more difficult.

8. Tongue-Twisters

Tongue-twisters are sets of words usually starting with the same letter. This makes them hard to recite clearly. They can be very useful in helping to learn good "articulation/enunciation/pronunciation." Radio announcers, lecturers and actors frequently use them to improve their attention to clear and correct speech. The longer twisters can be said through one time. The shorter ones are usually said through three times, the quicker the better. Reading tongue-twisters aloud is a good test of diction. Some individuals, however, may want to try to learn them by rote, in order to test their memories as well as their speech. Tongue-twisters are useful in helping to train the tongue. But the truth is that most people who become interested in tongue-twisters do so because they are just plain fun to try!

Rubber baby buggy bumpers.

A big black bug bit a big black bear.

She sells sea shells by the sea shore.

Six thick thistle sticks.

The slowly sinking ship sank.

Good blood, bad blood.

See the shy soldier.

Red leather, yellow leather.

Twenty tired twins thoughtfully twisting twine.

Six sick sheep.

Is this a zither?

Flesh of fresh flying fish.

One old Oxford ox opening oysters.

Fifty funny, fat, French friars fanning fainting flies.

Over the river ... a lump of raw liver.

145

Six sleek, slippery seals, slinking and sliding, slipped silently ashore.

Sister Susie's sewing shirts for soldiers.

Around rough and rugged rocks, the ragged rascal ran.

Sip a cup of proper coffee from a copper coffee pot.

A box of biscuits, a box of mixed biscuits, and a biscuit mixer.

Just how high would a horsefly fly, if a horsefly would fly high?

Of all the felt I ever felt, I never felt felt that felt like that felt felt.

She saw him saw six, slick, sleek, slim, slender, sycamore saplings.

See the Chief of the chief sheep section.

Greasy Granny grasped the great gray goose.

Five live hives ajive.

Pop and popped popcorn.

The Leith police dismisseth us, I'm thankful, sir, to say.

Ninety-nine nuns ran ninety-nine miles through ninety-nine towns in ninety-nine nightgowns.

Tom Tire tried to tie his tie twice.

If two witches were watching two watches, which witch would watch which watch?

The sun sure shines on the shiny sign.

Robert Rowley rolled a round ball round and round.

Amidst the mists with angry boasts,
He thrusts his fists against the posts,
And still insists he sees the ghosts.

Moses supposes his toesies are roses,
But Moses supposes erroneously,
For nobody's toesies are posies of roses,
As Moses supposes his toesies to be.

It's a quizzical quiz, kiss me quick.

Three little ghostesses sitting on postesses,
Eating buttered toastesses,
Greasing their fistesses up to the wristesses,
Oh what beastesses to make such feastesses.

The witch of Wibbleton and the witch of Wobbleton were watching each other whirl round the Wibbleton and Wobbleton watchtowers.

Men munch much mush, and women munch much mush.
Do men munch more mush or do women munch more mush?
Many men and women must munch much mush.

Three gray geese in the green grass grazing;
Gray were the geese and green was the grazing.

Eight great gray geese gazing and grazing,
Gazing and grazing were eight great gray geese,
Gazing and grazing gaily in Greece.

If one doctor doctors another doctor, does the doctor that's doctoring the doctor, doctor the doctor the way the doctor that's being doctored doctors, or does he doctor the doctor the way the doctor that's doctoring doctors?

The baboon blabbed and blubbered, dabbled in ribbons, gabbled in gibberish, played hob-nob with a robin, browbeat the tabby, made a hubbub for the rabble, bribed a nabob, and barbarously bamboozled a booby.

A bitter biting bittern bit a better brother bittern,
And the bitten better bittern bit the bitter biter back.
And the bitter bittern, bitten by the better bitten bittern,
Said, "I'm a bitter bittern biter bit by a better bittern a bit."

If a Hottentot tutor taught a Hottentot tot,
To talk ere the tot could totter,
Ought the Hottentot tot be taught
To say aught or naught,
Or what ought to be taught to the Hottentot tot,
By the Hottentot tutor who taught the tot
To talk ere the Hottentot tot could totter?

If you cross a cross across a cross,
Or cross a stick across a stick,
Or cross a stick across a cross,
Or cross a cross across a stick,
Or stick a stick across a stick,
Or stick a cross across a cross,
Or stick a cross across a stick,
Or stick a stick across a cross,
What kind of an acrostic would that be?

See the snow-white swan.
Swan swam over the sea,
Swim, swan, swim.
Swan swam back o'er the sea,
Well swam, swan,
Well swam over the sea.

How much wood would a woodchuck chuck if a woodchuck could chuck wood? He would chuck, he would, as much as he could, and chuck as much wood as a woodchuck would if a woodchuck could chuck wood.

Esau Wood sawed wood. All the wood Esau Wood saw, Esau Wood
would saw. All the wood Wood saw, Esau sought to saw. One day
Esau Wood's wood-saw would saw no wood. So Esau Wood sought a
new wood-saw. The new wood-saw would saw wood. Oh, the wood,
Esau Wood would saw. Esau sought a saw that would saw wood as
no other wood-saw would saw. And Esau found a saw that would
saw as no other wood-saw would saw. And Esau Wood sawed wood.

Theophilus Thadeus Thistledown, the successful thistle-sifter,
While sifting a sieve-full of unsifted thistles,
Thrust three thousand thistles through the thick of his thumb.
Now, if Theophilus Thadeus Thistledown, the successful thistle-sifter,
Thrust three thousand thistles through the thick of his thumb,
See that thou, while sifting a sieve-full of unsifted thistles,
Thrust not three thousand thistles through the thick of thy thumb.

Betty Botter bought some butter,
"But," she said, "this butter's bitter.
If I put it in my batter,
It will make my batter bitter.
But a bit of better butter,
Will but make my batter better."
So Betty Botter bought a bit of butter,
Better than the bitter butter.
She put a bit of the better butter,
Into her batter,
And it made the batter better,
So Betty Botter was glad she bought
The bit of better butter,
To maker her batter better,
Instead of using the bitter butter
To make her batter bitter.

Peter Piper's Alphabet

The original Peter Piper's Alphabet was first heard in England in the
mid-nineteenth century. The versions still existing today have a few
differences in the people who are in the tongue-twister alphabet, but
Peter Piper appears in almost the same way. The following is one version.

Andrew Airpump asked his aunt her ailment.
Did Andrew Airpump ask his aunt her ailment?
If Andrew Airpump asked his aunt her ailment,
Where's the ailment of Andrew Airpump's aunt?

Billy Button bought a buttered biscuit.
Did Billy Button buy a buttered biscuit?
If Billy Button bought a buttered biscuit,
Where's the buttered biscuit Billy Button bought?

Captain Crackskull cracked his cousin's cockscomb.
Did Captain Crackskull crack his cousin's cockscomb?
If Captain Crackskull cracked his cousin's cockscomb,
Where's the cousin's cockscomb Captain Crackskull cracked?

Davy Doldrum dreamed he drove a dragon.
Did Davy Doldrum dream he drove a dragon?
If Davy Doldrum dreamed he drove a dragon,
Where's the dragon Davy Doldrum dreamed he drove?

Enoch Eldridge ate an empty eggshell.
Did Enoch Eldridge eat an empty eggshell?
If Enoch Eldridge ate an empty eggshell,
Where's the empty eggshell Enoch Eldridge ate?

Francis Fribble flogged a Frenchman's filly.
Did Francis Fribble flog a Frenchman's filly?
If Francis Fribble flogged a Frenchman's filly,
Where's the Frenchman's filly Francis Fribble flogged?

Gaffer Gilpin got a goose and gander.
Did Gaffer Gilpin get a goose and gander?
If Gaffer Gilpin got a goose and gander,
Where's the goose and gander Gaffer Gilpin got?

Humphrey Hunchback had a hundred hedgehogs.
Did Humphrey Hunchback have a hundred hedgehogs?
If Humphrey Hunchback had a hundred hedgehogs,
Where's the hundred hedgehogs Humphrey Hunchback
    had?

Inigo Impey itched for an Indian image.
Did Inigo Impey itch for an Indian image?
If Inigo Impey itched for an Indian image,
Where's the Indian image Inigo Impey itched for?

Jumping Jacky jeered a jesting juggler.
Did Jumping Jacky jeer a jesting juggler?
If Jumping Jacky jeered a jesting juggler,
Where's the jesting juggler Jumping Jacky jeered?

Kimbo Kemble kicked his kinsman's kettle.
Did Kimbo Kemble kick his kinsman's kettle?
If Kimbo Kemble kicked his kinsman's kettle,
Where's the kinsman's kettle Kimbo Kemble kicked?

Lanky Lawrence lost his lass and lobster.
Did Lanky Lawrence lose his lass and lobster?
If Lanky Lawrence lost his lass and lobster,
Where are the lass and lobster Lanky Lawrence lost?

Matthew Mendlegs missed his mangled monkey.
Did Matthew Mendlegs miss his mangled monkey?
If Matthew Mendlegs missed his mangled monkey,
Where's the mangled monkey Matthew Mendlegs missed?

Neddy Noodle nipped his neighbor's nutmeg.
Did Neddy Noodle nip his neighbor's nutmeg?
If Neddy Noodle nipped his neighbor's nutmeg,
Where's the neighbor's nutmeg Neddy Noodle nipped?

Oliver Oglethorpe ogled an owl and oyster.
Did Oliver Oglethorpe ogle an owl and oyster?
If Oliver Oglethorpe ogled an owl and oyster,
Where are the owl and oyster Oliver Oglethorpe ogled?

Peter Piper picked a peck of pickled pepper.
Did Peter Piper pick a peck of pickled pepper?
If Peter Piper picked a peck of pickled pepper,
Where's the peck of pickled pepper Peter Piper picked?

Questing Quicksight quizzed a queerish question.
Did Questing Quicksight quiz a queerish question?
If Questing Quicksight quizzed a queerish question,
Where's the queerish question Questing Quicksight
    quizzed?

Rory Rumpus rode a rawboned racer.
Did Rory Rumpus ride a rawboned racer?
If Rory Rumpus rode a rawboned racer,
Where's the rawboned racer Rory Rumpus rode?

Sammy Smellie smelled a smell of smelts.
Did Sammy Smellie smell a smell of smelts?
If Sammy Smellie smelled a smell of smelts,
Where's the smell of smelts Sammy Smellie smelled?

Tiptoe Tommy turned a Turk for twopence.
Did Tiptoe Tommy turn a Turk for twopence?
If Tiptoe Tommy turned a Turk for twopence,
Where's the Turk for twopence Tiptoe Tommy turned?

Uncle Usher urged an ugly urchin.
Did Uncle Usher urge an ugly urchin?
If Uncle Usher urged an ugly urchin,
Where's the ugly urchin Uncle Usher urged?

Vincent Veedom veered his vast vehicle.
Did Vincent Veedom veer his vast vehicle?
If Vincent Veedom veered his vast vehicle,
Where's the vast vehicle Vincent Veedom veered?

Walter Waddle won a walking wager.
Did Walter Waddle win a walking wager?
If Walter Waddle won a walking wager,
Where's the walking wager Walter Waddle won?

X Y Z ended with x y z.
Did X Y Z end with x y z?
If X Y Z ended with x y z,
Where are the x y z X Y Z ended with?

Cumulative Counting-Twisters

Cumulative counting-twisters can be done by one person or played with a leader and group. There are two ways to use them as group play. In the first, the leader would give the new line and point to an individual who is to recite. In the second, the entire group responds together. The leader gives each new line to the group and they repeat the sets together. Either way it is played, the counting-twister is recited by accumulating verses and repeating them all from the beginning as each new one is added. Example: Line 1. Line 1 + 2. Line 1 + 2 + 3. Line 1 + 2 + 3 + 4, etc., until the entire set is included. Players may also wish to invent their own cumulative counting-twisters.

Easy Animals

1. One old owl.
2. Two tiny toads.
3. Three thriving thrushes.
4. Four frolicking fawns.
5. Five fine fish.
6. Six slinky snakes.

7. Seven slithering seals.   9. Nine nesting nightingales.
8. Eight eager eagles.   10. Ten terrible tigers.
                                      — *Gloria T. Delamar.*

For additional fun and practice, say each line three times before saying the next line!

Five-Word Cumulative

1. One orphan ostrich ogling orioles.
2. Two toddlers toddling to town.
3. Three thieves thumping thick things.
4. Four fat frogs furiously frowning.
5. Five fiddlers fiddling fancy fiddlesticks.
6. Six shovelers shoveling soft snow.
7. Seven salty sailors sailing south.
8. Eight enormous elephants eating everything.
9. Nine natives napping near neighbors.
10. Ten tired turtles topsy turvy.
                                      — *Gloria T. Delamar.*

Players may want to say each of these lines three times to make the recitation of the tongue-twister harder.

A note: When playing in groups, players should agree beforehand whether or not a mistake will put a player out of the game. They can decide that one mistake puts a player out or that a player is out after making three mistakes. If the group has younger players along with more experienced ones, they may decide that nobody needs to drop out of the game because of mistakes.

Alphabet Tongue-Twister Game

This is a game in which a group of players can create their own alphabet tongue-twisters. Each letter of the alphabet is put on a separate piece of paper. (It is suggested that X, Y, and Z be eliminated.) Players all draw one or more letters from a table or box, depending on how many people are playing. Each player should have the same number of letters. (Just leave extra papers in the box.) Each player then makes a tongue-twister sentence from his letter. Set a time limit; five minutes for one letter, 10 minutes for two letters, and 15 minutes for three letters. The one making the longest sentence wins. If more than one sentence is made by each player, add up all the words of all the sentences to determine the winner.

Examples: M = Melancholy Melissa missed mailing more merry

mistletoe to misty marble mansions. (Ten words.) (Players are allowed to add a few little words like *and*, *from*, *the*, etc., to join the letter-words.) W = Whispering, whiskery Walter waited, watching warily while wild, whopping Will wantonly whipped the weary, whining, wailing, walrus and weak, whimpering, white whale with well-water west of Wessex wharf. (25 words.)

Follow-Up Game

After the sentences have been made, another game of reading them aloud can follow. Each person draws a tongue-twister from the box and must read it aloud quickly three times. Players should try to write clearly! (Those whose handwriting is not legible, may be forced to read their own aloud!)

9. "Staircase" Tales

"Staircase" tales are most effective as experiments in "visualization." The people, animals and events change very rapidly from sentence to sentence. This makes them ideal for creating pictures in one's mind. Conscious attention to visualization can help to enrich an individual's abilities.

Doing these tales, and visualizations, with a group might provoke some interesting discussion. Were a person's images in color or in black-and-white? What were the people wearing? Could they actually see faces? Were they faces of people they knew or made-up of features they felt belonged to that particular type of character? Were the pictures still or in motion? The differences in what and how people visualize provide a fascinating lesson in personalities.

"Staircase" stories do not have a plot, but they do involve cause and effect. Some of those included here are double-staircase stories, in that they not only go up the tale, but then run back down again. In this chapter, too, are "escalator" or "repeater" tales, whose ends lead back to their beginnings. There are also a number of "Stumbling-Steps," which are word tricks to play on "victims."

The House That Jack Built

This is the house that Jack built.

This is the malt,
That lay in the house that Jack built.

This is the rat,
That ate the malt,
That lay in the house that Jack built.

This is the cat,
That killed the rat,
That ate the malt,
That lay in the house that Jack built.

This is the dog,
That worried the cat,
That killed the rat,
That ate the malt,
That lay in the house that Jack built.

This is the cow with the crumpled horn,
That tossed the dog,
That worried the cat,
That killed the rat,
That ate the malt,
That lay in the house that Jack built.

This is the maiden all forlorn,
That milked the cow with the crumpled horn,
That tossed the dog,
That worried the cat,
That killed the rat,
That ate the malt,
That lay in the house that Jack built.

This is the man all tattered and torn,
That kissed the maiden all forlorn,
That milked the cow with the crumpled horn,
That tossed the dog,
That worried the cat,
That killed the rat,
That ate the malt,
That lay in the house that Jack built.

This is the priest all shaven and shorn,
That married the man all tattered and torn,
That kissed the maiden all forlorn,
That milked the cow with the crumpled horn,
That tossed the dog,
That worried the cat,
That killed the rat,
That ate the malt,
That lay in the house that Jack built.

This is the cock the crowed in the morn,
That waked the priest all shaven and shorn,
That married the man all tattered and torn,
That kissed the maiden all forlorn,
That milked the cow with the crumpled horn,
That tossed the dog,

That worried the cat,
That killed the rat,
That ate the malt,
That lay in the house that Jack built.

This is the farmer that sowed his corn,
That kept the cock that crowed in the morn,
That waked the priest all shaven and shorn,
That married the man all tattered and torn,
That kissed the maiden all forlorn,
That milked the cow with the crumpled horn,
That tossed the dog,
That worried the cat,
That killed the rat,
That ate the malt,
That lay in the house that Jack built.

This is the end of a tale that was born,
About ... the farmer that sowed his corn,
That kept the cock that crowed in the morn,
That waked the priest all shaven and shorn,
That married the man all tattered and torn,
That kissed the maiden all forlorn,
That milked the cow with the crumpled horn,
That tossed the dog,
That worried the cat,
That killed the rat,
That ate the malt,
That lay in the house that Jack built.
— Mother Goose tale.

The Crooked Man

There was a crooked man,
And he walked a crooked mile.
He found a crooked sixpence,
Against a crooked stile.
He bought a crooked cat,
Which caught a crooked mouse,
And they all lived together
In a little crooked house.
— Mother Goose rhyme.

For Want of a Nail

For want of a nail
    The shoe was lost.
For want of a shoe
    The horse was lost.
For want of a horse
    The rider was lost.
For want of a rider
    The battle was lost.
For want of a battle
    The kingdom was lost.
And all for the want
    Of a horse-shoe nail.
                —Author unknown.

The Key to the Kingdom

This is the key to the kingdom.
In the kingdom there is a city.
In the city there is a town.
In the town there is a street.
In the street there is a yard.
In the yard there is a house.
In the house there is a room.
In the room there is a bed.
On the bed there is a basket.
In the basket there are flowers.
    Flowers in the basket,
    Basket on the bed,
    Bed in the room,
    Room in the house,
    House in the yard,
    Yard in the street,
    Street in the town,
    Town in the city,
    City in the kingdom...
And this is the key to the kingdom.
                —Author unknown.

Big-Bellied-Ben

Benjamin Benjamin, Big-Bellied-Ben;
He ate more meat than a hundred men.

He ate a calf, he ate a cow,
He ate a lamb, he ate a sow.

He ate a rooster, he ate a hen,
He ate a crow, he ate a wren.

He ate a duck, he ate a goose,
He ate a deer, he ate a moose.

He ate a wolf, he ate a bear,
He ate a squirrel, he ate a hare.

He ate a goat, he ate a horse,
Then he called for more to eat, of course!

He ate a church, he ate the steeple,
He ate the priest, he ate the people!

A calf and a cow,
A lamb and a sow,
A rooster and a hen,
A crow and a wren,
A duck and a goose,
A deer and a moose,
A wolf and a bear,
A squirrel and a hare,
A goat and a horse,
And more, of course!
A church and a steeple,
The priest and the people!

Big-Bellied-Ben, ate all he could get,
And then complained, he wasn't full yet.

*— adapted from a Mother Goose
rhyme and enlarged,
by Gloria T. Delamar.*

The Old Woman and Her Pig

An old woman was sweeping her house, and she found a sixpence.
"What shall I do with this sixpence?" she said.
"I know. I will go to market and buy a little pig."
So she went to the market and she bought a little pig. On the way home,
    they came to a stile.

But the pig would not go over the stile.
She went a little farther, and she met a dog.
So she said to the dog,
    "Dog, dog, bite pig!
    Pig won't go over the stile,
    And I shan't get home tonight."
But the dog would not.
She went a little farther, and she met a stick.
So she said to the stick,
    "Stick, stick, beat dog!
    Dog won't bite pig,
    Pig won't go over the stile,
    And I shan't get home tonight."
But the stick would not.
She went a little farther, and she met a fire.
So she said to the fire,
    "Fire, fire, burn stick!
    Stick won't beat dog,
    Dog won't bite pig,
    Pig won't go over the stile,
    And I shan't get home tonight."
But the fire would not.
She went a little farther, and she met some water.
So she said to the water,
    "Water, water, quench fire!
    Fire won't burn stick,
    Stick won't beat dog,
    Dog won't bite pig,
    Pig won't go over the stile,
    And I shan't get home tonight."
But the water would not.
She went a little farther, and she met an ox.
So she said to the ox,
    "Ox, ox, drink water!
    Water won't quench fire,
    Fire won't burn stick,
    Stick won't beat dog,
    Dog won't bite pig,
    Pig won't go over the stile,
    And I shan't get home tonight."
But the ox would not.
She went a little farther, and she met a butcher.
So she said to the butcher,
    "Butcher, butcher, kill ox!
    Ox won't drink water,
    Water won't quench fire,

Fire won't burn stick,
Stick won't beat dog,
Dog won't bite pig,
Pig won't go over the stile,
And I shan't get home tonight."
But the butcher would not.
She went a little farther, and she met a rope.
So she said to the rope,
"Rope, rope, hang butcher!
Butcher won't kill ox,
Ox won't drink water,
Water won't quench fire,
Fire won't burn stick,
Stick won't beat dog,
Dog won't bite pig,
Pig won't go over the stile,
And I shan't get home tonight."
But the rope would not.
She went a little farther, and she met a rat.
So she said to the rat,
"Rat, rat, gnaw rope!
Rope won't hang butcher,
Butcher won't kill ox,
Ox won't drink water,
Water won't quench fire,
Fire won't burn stick,
Stick won't beat dog,
Dog won't bite pig,
Pig won't go over the stile,
And I shan't get home tonight."
But the rat would not.
She went a little farther, and she met a cat.
So she said to the cat,
"Cat, cat, kill rat!
Rat won't gnaw rope,
Rope won't hang butcher,
Butcher won't kill ox,
Ox won't drink water,
Water won't quench fire,
Fire won't burn stick,
Stick won't beat dog,
Dog won't bite pig,
Pig won't go over the stile,
And I shan't get home tonight."
And the cat said to her,

"If you will go over to the cow in the next field and fetch me a
    saucer of milk, I will kill the rat."
So the old woman went over to the cow in the next field.
And the cow said to her,
"If you will go over to the haystack and fetch me a handful of
    hay, I will give you the milk."
So the old woman went over to the haystack to fetch a handful of hay
    for the cow. After the cow had eaten the hay, she gave the old
    woman the milk.
The old woman went back to the cat with the milk in a saucer.
As soon as the cat had lapped up the milk —
    The cat began to kill the rat —
    The rat began to gnaw the rope —
    The rope began to hang the butcher —
    The butcher began to kill the ox —
    The ox began to drink the water —
    The water began to quench the fire —
    The fire began to burn the stick —
    The stick began to beat the dog —
    The dog began to bite the pig —
    The pig jumped over the stile —
And the old woman got home that night!

— Mother Goose tale.

The Cock on the Rock

A crowing cock sat on a rock
And woke the lighthouse-keeper,
Who called aloud into the night,
Which gave his little dog a fright.
The little dog ran round the house,
Which set the bull to roaring.
Which drove the monkey in the boat,
Who set the oars a-rowing,
And scared the cock upon the rock
Who cracked his throat with crowing.

— Author unknown (adapted).

What Happened Because
of a Sleepy Chick

One morning a certain boy-chick woke up feeling rather grumpy
    because he hadn't had enough sleep.

When his sister asked him what time it was, he didn't make a peep.
Now, sister-chick didn't know the time; she got to breakfast late.
That made mother-hen upset, and she fussed and knocked over a plate.
The plate fell onto father-rooster's head, just as he remembered his
    son in the bed.
So, his crowing call sounded angry as he said, "Where are you?"
And the boy-chick whimpered, "Now what did I do?"

                     — Gloria T. Delamar.

The Kitchen Riot

The kitchen clock began to toll,
As the spatula beat the bowl.

The cups and saucers rattled,
The scrub-brush and dishpan battled.

The stove gave a blast of fire,
The dishrag hung from a wire.

The knife and fork had a duel,
The frying pan pushed over the stool.

The plate jumped up on the table,
To see the pot swallow the ladle.

The broom that stood behind the door,
Threw the pudding-stick on the floor.

Said the gridiron, "Can't they agree?
I'm the head constable, bring them to me.

    The kitchen clock that began to toll,
    The spatula that beat the bowl.

    The cups and saucers that rattled,
    The scrub-brush and dishpan that battled.

    The knife and fork that had a duel,
    The frying pan that pushed over the stool.

    The plate that jumped up on the table,
    The pot that swallowed the ladle.

    The broom that stood behind the door,
    That threw the pudding-stick on the floor."

The gridiron bade them all be quiet,
And that was the end of the kitchen riot.
> *— adapted from a Mother Goose*
> *rhyme and enlarged,*
> *by Gloria T. Delamar.*

The Share in the Air

What is that?
    It is a chest.
What is in the chest?
    Gold and silver.
Where is my share?
    The mouse ran away with it.
Where is the mouse?
    In her house.
Where is her house?
    In the forest.
Where is the forest?
    The fire burnt it.
Where is the fire?
    The water quenched it.
Where is the water?
    The bull drank it.
Where is the bull?
    Behind the hill.
Where is the hill?
    Covered with snow.
Where is the snow?
    The sun melted it.
Where is the sun?
    High, high,
    High up in the air!
> *—Author unknown.*

The Tree of the Forest

This is the Tree of the forest.

This is the Ax whose steady blows
Cut down the Tree of the forest.

This is the Woodman, who, everyone knows,
Wielded the Ax whose steady blows
Cut down the Tree of the forest.

This is the Log—to the river's side
Rolled by the Woodman, who, everyone knows,
Wielded the Ax whose steady blows
Cut down the Tree of the forest.

This is the River whose flowing tide
Carried the Log that was rolled to its side, —
Rolled by the Woodman, who, everyone knows,
Wielded the Ax whose steady blows
Cut down the Tree of the forest.

This is the Wheel that went whirring round,
Turned by the River whose flowing tide
Carried the Log that was rolled to its side, —
Rolled by the Woodman, who, everyone knows,
Wielded the Ax whose steady blows
Cut down the Tree of the forest.

These are the Saws which, with buzzing sound,
Were moved by the Wheel that went whirring round,
Turned by the River whose flowing tide
Carried the Log that was rolled to its side, —
Rolled by the Woodman, who, everyone knows,
Wielded the Ax whose heavy blows
Cut down the Tree of the forest.

These are the Boards, so straight and long,
Cut by the Saws which, with buzzing sound,
Were moved by the Wheel that went whirring round,
Turned by the River whose flowing tide
Carried the Log that was rolled to its side, —
Rolled by the Woodman, who, everyone knows,
Wielded the Ax whose heavy blows
Cut down the Tree of the forest.

This is the Carpenter, skillful and strong,
Who planed all the Boards so straight and long,
Cut by the Saws which, with buzzing sound,
Were moved by the Wheel that went whirring round,
Turned by the River whose flowing tide
Carried the Log that was rolled to its side, —
Rolled by the Woodman, who, everyone knows,
Wielded the Ax whose steady blows
Cut down the Tree of the forest.

This is the House with its windows and doors
With timbers and rafters and roofs and floors,

Which was built by the Carpenter skillful and strong
Who planed all the Boards so straight and long,
Cut by the Saws which, with buzzing sound,
Were moved by the Wheel that went whirring round,
Turned by the River whose flowing tide
Carried the Log that was rolled to its side, —
Rolled by the Woodman, who, everyone knows,
Wielded the Ax whose steady blows
Cut down the Tree of the forest.

This is the Family — All are here —
Father, and mother and children dear,
Who live in the House with windows and doors,
With timbers and rafters and roofs and floors,
Which was built by the Carpenter, skillful and strong,
Who planed all the Boards so straight and long,
Cut by the Saws which, with buzzing sound,
Were moved by the Wheel that went whirring round,
Turned by the River whose flowing tide
Carried the Log that was rolled to its side, —
Rolled by the Woodman, who, everyone knows,
Wielded the Ax whose steady blows
Cut down the Tree of the forest.

— Emilie Poulsson. *

"Escalator" or Repeater Tales

The rhythm, pattern and trickery of repeater stories is illustrated in the ones which are included here. Although not strictly "staircase" stories, they can easily be considered "escalator" tales. They consist of a chain of events which eventually link back to the beginning. Just as the cable of an escalator moves the steps in an endless circle, so too, do these stories go around and around in repetition.

Pete and Re-Peat

Pete had a twin brother.
His brother's name was Re-Peat.
One day, Pete and his brother were sitting on a wall
    and Pete fell off.

Who was left?

Re-Peat!

*In the Child's World, 1893.

Pete had a twin brother.
His brother's name was Re-Peat
One day, Pete and his brother were sitting on a
    wall and Pete fell off.

Who was left?

Repeat!

Pete had a twin brother, etc.

(This can also be done as a "stumbling step" to trick someone. Tell the story to someone and wait for their answer after asking, "Who was left?")

Hoodoo

"You remind me of a man."
    "What man?"

"A man with power."
    "What power?"

"The power to Hoodoo."
    "Hoodoo?"

"You do."
    "Do what?"

"You remind me of a man."
    "What man?" ... etc.

Three Questions Without Answers

These questions are "repeaters" because trying to figure out the answers to them will keep you going round and round, and because the answers themselves go round and round!

1. Which came first; the chicken or the egg?

2. Where does a lap go when a person stands up?

3. Which goes through a board first; a bullet or the
    hole?

The Mate's Tale

It was a dark and stormy night.
The wind was howling and the rain was pouring down.
The ocean was in an uproar, and the waves were fifty feet high.
The ship tossed and pitched, up and down, from side to side.
It rocked and rolled in every direction.

The sailors were getting restless, so the captain called his crew together.
They all gathered around.
Meanwhile, the storm raged.
They could see and feel the wind whip the water against the side of the
    ship.
They shivered with cold and fear, knowing the dangers of a storm at sea.

The captain knew he must make them think of something else.
If he didn't, there might soon be panic aboard.
He looked his first mate sternly in the eye.
The captain said the mate, "Mate, tell us a story."
So the mate began:

> "It was a dark and stormy night.
> The wind was howling and the rain was pouring down.
> The ocean was in an uproar, and the waves were fifty feet high.
> The ship tossed and pitched, up and down, from side to side.
> It rocked and rolled in every direction.
>
> The sailors were getting restless, so the captain called his crew
>   together.
> They all gathered around.
> Meanwhile, the storm raged.
> They could see and feel the wind whip the water against the side
>   of the ship.
> They shivered with cold and fear, knowing the dangers of a storm
>   at sea.
>
> The captain knew he must make them think of something else.
> If he didn't, there might soon be panic aboard.
> He looked his first mate sternly in the eye.
> The captain said to the mate, "Mate, tell us a story."
> So the mate began:
>
>> 'It was a dark and stormy night ... etc.'"
>>   *—Gloria T. Delamar.*

How the Indian Boy Chooses a Name

How does the Indian boy choose a name?
That makes him brave in any game?
He says there is the E
 N
  D
   less-Archer, and the Darting-
           Spear;
Sitting-Bull, Almighty-Bear and Running-Deer;
Thunder-Cloud, Quick-Shooting-Star and Silver-Moon;
Rain-in-Face, Eyes-to-the-Sun and Singing-Loon;
Leaping-Lizard, Creeping-Fox and Snake-that-Flies;
Dreaming-Rabbit, Howling-Wolf and Owl-so-Wise;
Hawkeye, Eagle-Feather, and Greening-Leaf;
A
 N
  D
   then he goes to ask his Indian Chief....

How does the Indian boy choose a name?
That makes him brave in any game?
He says there is the E
 N
  D
   less-Archer, and the
           Darting-Spear;
Sitting-Bull, Almighty-Bear and Running Deer;
Thunder-Cloud, Quick-Shooting-Star and Silver-
       Moon;
Rain-in-Face, Eyes-to-the-Sun and Singing-Loon;
Leaping-Lizard, Creeping-Fox and Snake-that-Flies;
Dreaming-Rabbit, Howling-Wolf and Owl-so-Wise;
Hawkeye, Eagle-Feather, and Greening-Leaf;
A
 N
  D
   then he goes to ask his Indian Chief....

How does the Indian boy choose a name?
That makes him brave in any game?
He says there is the E
 N
  D
   !!!!!!!!!!
        — *Gloria T. Delamar.*

A Bear Went over a Mountain

A bear went over a mountain,
A bear went over a mountain,
A bear went over a mountain,
And what do you think he saw?

He saw another mountain,
He saw another mountain,
He saw another mountain,
And what do you think he did?

He climbed the other mountain,
He climbed the other mountain,
He climbed the other mountain,
And what do you think he saw?

He saw another mountain, etc.
He climbed another mountain, etc.

(Alternately repeat; He saw another mountain, etc. and He climbed another mountain, etc.)

(At end: after "And what do you think he did?")

He fell fast asleep.
Why, why, why?
Because he had climbed so many mountains!

"Stumbling Steps"

"Stumbling Steps" are word tricks to play on "victims." The person playing the trick can choose another person to be the victim or he can play the trick on several people and the one who is caught by the "stumbling step" will be the victim. Most people think it is rather funny to "stumble" over these word tricks and to be caught!

I Am a Gold Lock

Instructions from leader: Repeat everything that I say, except you are to say the word "key" where I say the word "lock.

I am a gold lock.
I am a gold key.

I am a silver lock.
    I am a silver key.
I am a brass lock.
    I am a brass key.
I am a lead lock.
    I am a lead key.
I am a monk lock.
    I am a monk-key! (Victim.)

Just Like Me

Instructions from leader: All you have to do is say "Just like me" after everything I say.

I went up one pair of stairs.
    Just like me.
I went up two pair of stairs.
    Just like me.
I went into a room.
    Just like me.
I looked out of the window.
    Just like me.
And there I saw a monkey.
    Just like me! (Victim.)

The Old Dead Horse

Instructions from leader: Repeat what I say, but say one number higher each time.

I saw an old dead horse. I one it.
I saw an old dead horse. I two it.
I saw an old dead horse. I three it.
I saw an old dead horse. I four it.
I saw an old dead horse. I five it.
I saw an old dead horse. I six it.
I saw an old dead horse. I seven it.
I saw an old dead horse. I eight (ate) it! (Victim.)

Say "Black"

I bet I can make you say "black."
    How?

Well, what are the colors of the flag?
　　Red, white, and blue.
See, I knew I could make you say "blue."
　　You didn't say "blue," you said "black." (Victim.)
Yes, but you just said "black!"

Say Your Favorite Color Twice

I bet I can make you say your favorite color twice.
　　I bet you can't.
Well, first, what's your favorite color?
　　Green. (Or whatever the victim says.)
What? (Pretend not to have heard — if necessary, say
　　"I couldn't understand you.")
　　Green. (Victim.)
Ha, ha, ha, you just said it the second time!

An Intelligence Test

Do you want to take an intelligence test?
　　Okay.
Well, here's a question for you. Without checking to
　　look, now...
What is the color of your eyes?
　　Blue. (Or whatever the victim answers.)
Okay, then next, what is the color of your hair?
　　Brown.
What is the color of your shirt? (Or dress, or sweater,
　　or whatever.)
　　White. (You can also add pants, skirt, hat, etc.)
What color are your socks? (If victim is wearing socks.)
　　Black.
What color are your shoes?
　　Brown.
Uh, let's see now, what was the first question I asked you?
　　What is the color of your eyes? (Victim.)
No, it wasn't. The first question was "Do you want to
　　take an intelligence test?" (and the victim has been
　　caught).

Another version of the above "intelligence test" is:

Do you want to take an intelligence test?
　　Okay.

What is your name?
> (Victim answers, telling his name.)

How old are you?
> (Victim answers.)

What color are your eyes?
> (Victim answers.)

How many fingers do you have?
> (Victim answers.)

Let's see ... how many questions was that?
> *Four.* (Victim.)

No, it wasn't, that was the fifth question. The first one
was "Do you want to take an intelligence test?"
(and the victim has been caught).

The Bus

How are you at arithmetic? Can you add and subtract? (The victim says
yes, and then you start.)

Well, pretend you're a bus driver. At the first stop, 4 people get on the
bus. At the next stop 3 more people get on and 3 get off. At the next,
5 get on and 1 gets off. (Keep this up, adding and subtracting numbers as you go on. At some stops, people get on. At others some get
off. At some, there are people who get on and also people who get
off.)

(All the time you are giving the numbers, the victim will be keeping track
of the numbers and adding and subtracting in his head.)

Okay. Are you ready for the question? (Victim will say "yes" or nod.)
This is the question: "How old was the bus driver?"

Even the victims that remember *they* were the bus driver, will still be
caught by doing all that mental arithmetic!

Herman, the Magic Flea

Do you believe in Herman, the Magic Flea? (Hold out palm as though
holding "Herman" on it.)
> No. (Victim.)

Well, you just watch. (Pretend to put Herman down, then extend index
finger, holding it up high.)

"Jump over my finger Herman!"

"Well, he didn't make it. Here, hold his coat." (Pass "coat" to victim, who
usually goes through the motions of taking it.)

"Okay, jump over my finger now, Herman!"
"Oh dear, he still didn't make it. Here, hold his pants." (Pass "pants to
   victim.)
"Okay, Herman, jump over my finger now."
"Hooray! He made it!"
Now do you believe in Herman, the Magic Flea?
     No. (Victim.)
Then why are you holding his coat and pants?!!!

Touching or Not?

(Before you start, get yourself into a position where you can casually
touch the victim on one arm or gently have your arm around his shoulder.)
Say: "Watch this."
(Slowly bring your index finger very close to the victim's hand, but do not
actually touch his hand with the finger.)
Ask: "Am I touching you?"
     No. (the victim almost never "catches on" and answers "no.")
Yes I am!!! (pat victim with hand that was touching him all the time!)

Do You Know How to Play Rabbit?

This is a stunt to play on a whole group of victims. When the group is in
the right mood, spring this on them with enthusiasm and you will be able
to victimize them all!

Hey, do you know how to play rabbit? (People will say "no" and before
   they have a chance to ask questions about it, you get them started.)
Tell them:
Everybody get down on the floor on their knees in a circle.

Okay, now sit back on your heels and lean your head forward. Hold out
   your hands like rabbit paws.

Now, one at a time, around the circle, repeat the phrases.

Leader speaks to person at his left. Pat the floor with "paws" while speaking. "Do you know how to play rabbit?"

Player is to answer, "No, I don't know how to play rabbit." (Give whatever instructions seem necessary.)

(Player is to pat floor with "paws" when he answers and also when he
   asks the question of the next player to his left.)

"Do you know how to play rabbit?"

All around the circle so that everyone has a chance:
"No, I don't know how to play rabbit." (To player on right.)
"Do you know how to play rabbit?" (To player on left.)

When the last person, the one to the right of the leader says, "Do you
know how to play rabbit?" to the leader, the leader jumps back up
and says to the group:
Well, if no one knows how to play rabbit, I guess we can't play!!!

10. Narrative Verses

Narrative verses have a special place in the area of stories. They tell a tale in rhymed sets of verses rather than with straight narration. Although all stories have their own rhythms, narrative verse follows a definite rhythmic beat. The particular selections included here are all classical pieces which have given pleasure to both children and adults since they were first written, many, many years ago.

The Wren Hunt

Let's go to the woods, says Robbin to Bobbin.
Let's go to the woods, says Bobbin to Robbin.
Let's go to the woods, says John all alone.
Let's go to the woods, says everyone.

Oh, what to do there? says Robbin to Bobbin.
Oh, what to do there; says Bobbin to Robbin.
Oh, what to do there? says John all alone.
Oh, what to do there? says everyone.

We'll hunt us a wren, says Robbin to Bobbin.
We'll hunt us a wren, says Bobbin to Robbin.
We'll hunt us a wren, says John all alone.
We'll hunt us a wren, says everyone.

Oh, I see a wren, says Robbin to Bobbin.
Oh, I see a wren, says Bobbin to Robbin.
Oh, I see a wren, says John all alone.
Oh, I see a wren, says everyone.

Let's shoot at the wren, says Robbin to Bobbin.
Let's shoot at the wren, says Bobbin to Robbin.
Let's shoot at the wren, says John all alone.
Let's shoot at the wren, says everyone.

She's down, she's down, says Robbin to Bobbin.
She's down, she's down, says Bobbin to Robbin.
She's down, she's down, says John all alone.
She's down, she's down, says everyone.

She's dead, she's dead, says Robbin to Bobbin.
She's dead, she's dead, says Bobbin to Robbin.
She's dead, she's dead, says John all alone.
She's dead, she's dead, says everyone.

Then pounce, then pounce, says Robbin to Bobbin.
Then pounce, then pounce, says Bobbin to Robbin.
Then pounce, then pounce, says John all alone.
Then pounce, then pounce, says everyone.

How to get it home? says Robbin to Bobbin.
How to get it home; says Bobbin to Robbin.
How to get it home? says John all alone.
How to get it home? says everyone.

With a cart and six horses, says Robbin to Bobbin.
With a cart and six horses, says Bobbin to Robbin.
With a cart and six horses, says John all alone.
With a cart and six horses, says everyone.

Then hoist her up, says Robbin to Bobbin.
Then hoist her up, says Bobbin to Robbin.
Then hoist her up, says John all alone.
Then hoist her up, says everyone.

Oh, who will cook it? says Robbin to Bobbin.
Oh, who will cook it? says Bobbin to Robbin.
Oh, who will cook it? says John all alone.
Oh, who will cook it? says everyone.

Oh, I will cook it, says Robbin to Bobbin.
Oh, I will cook it, says Bobbin to Robbin.
Oh, I will cook it, says John all alone.
Oh, I will cook it, says everyone.

How will we boil her? says Robbin to Bobbin.
How will we boil her? says Bobbin to Robbin.
How will we boil her? says John all alone.
How will we boil her? says everyone.

In the biggest pot, says Robbin to Bobbin.
In the biggest pot, says Bobbin to Robbin.
In the biggest pot, says John all alone.
In the biggest pot, says everyone.

Oh, who will eat it? says Robbin to Bobbin.
Oh, who will eat it? says Bobbin to Robbin.
Oh, who will eat it? says John all alone.
Oh, who will eat it? says everyone.

We'll all of us eat it, says Robbin to Bobbin.
We'll all of us eat it, says Bobbin to Robbin.
We'll all of us eat it, says John all alone.
We'll all of us eat it, says everyone.

What to do with the bones? says Robbin to Bobbin.
What to do with the bones? says Bobbin to Robbin.
What to do with the bones? says John all alone.
What to do with the bones? says everyone.

Leave the bones for the crows, says Robbin to Bobbin.
Leave the bones for the crows, says Bobbin to Robbin.
Leave the bones for the crows, says John all alone.
Leave the bones for the crows, says everyone.

Oh, what a good wren hunt, says Robbin to Bobbin.
Oh, what a good wren hunt, says Bobbin to Robbin.
Oh, what a good wren hunt, says John all alone.
Oh, what a good wren hunt, says everyone.
                                    — *Old folk tale.*

Old Mother Hubbard

Old Mother Hubbard
Went to the cupboard,
To get her poor dog a bone;
But when she got there
The cupboard was bare,
And so the poor dog had none.

She went to the baker's
To buy him some bread;
But when she came back
The poor dog was dead.

She went to the carpenter's
To buy him a coffin;
But when she came back
The poor dog was laughing.

She took a clean dish
To get him some tripe;
But when she came back
He was smoking a pipe.

She went to the fish-house
To buy him some fish;
But when she came back
He was licking the dish.

She went to the ale-house
To get him some beer;
But when she came back
The dog sat in a chair.

She went to the tavern
For white wine and red;
But when she came back
The dog stood on his head.

She went to the fruiterer's
To buy him some fruit;
But when she came back
He was playing a flute.

She went to the hatter's
To buy him a hat;
But when she came back
He was feeding the cat.

She went to the barber's
To buy him a wig;
But when she came back
He was dancing a jig.

She went to the tailor's
To buy him a coat;
But when she came back
He was riding a goat.

She went to the cobbler's
To buy him some shoes;
But when she came back
He was reading the news.

She went to the seamstress
To buy him some linen;
But when she came back
The dog was spinning.

She went to the hosier's
To buy him some hose;
But when she came back
He was dressed in his clothes.

The dame made a curtsey,
The dog made a bow;
The dame said, "Your servant,"
The dog said, "Bow-wow."

This wonderful dog
Was Dame Hubbard's delight;
He could sing, he could dance,
He could read, he could write.

She gave him rich dainties
Whenever he fed,
And erected a monument
When he was dead.

— *Mother Goose tale.*

Three Little Kittens

Three little kittens lost their mittens;
And they began to cry,
"Oh, mother dear,
We very much fear
That we have lost our mittens."

"Lost your mittens!
You naughty kittens!
Then you shall have no pie!"
    "Mee-ow, mee-ow, mee-ow,"
"No, you shall have no pie."

The three little kittens found their mittens;
    And they began to cry,
        "Oh, mother dear,
        See here, see here!
    See, we have found our mittens!"
        "Put on your mittens,
        You silly kittens,
    And you may have some pie."
        "Purr-r, purr-r, purr-r,
    Oh, let us have the pie!
        Purr-r, purr-r, purr-r."

The three little kittens put on their mittens,
    And soon ate up the pie;
        "Oh, mother dear,
        We greatly fear
    That we have soiled our mittens!"
        "Soiled your mittens!
        You naughty kittens!"
    Then they began to sigh,
        "Mee-ow, mee-ow, mee-ow."

The three little kittens washed their mittens,
    And hung them out to dry;
        "Oh, mother dear,
        Do you not hear
    That we have washed our mittens?"
        "Washed your mittens!
        Oh, you're good kittens!
    But I smell a rat close by;
        Hush, hush! Mee-ow, mee-ow."
    "We smell a rat close by,
        Mee-ow, mee-ow, mee-ow."
                        —*Author unknown.*

Mary's Lamb

Mary had a little lamb,
    Its fleece was white as snow;

And everywhere that Mary went
 The lamb was sure to go.

He followed her to school one day;
 That was against the rule;
It made the children laugh and play
 To see a lamb at school.

And so the teacher turned him out,
 But still he lingered near,
And waited patiently about
 Till Mary did appear.

Then he ran to her, and laid
 His head upon her arm,
As if he said, "I'm not afraid—
 You'll keep me from all harm."

"What makes the lamb love Mary so?"
 The eager children cry.
"Oh, Mary loves the lamb, you know,"
 The teacher did reply.

And you each gentle animal
 In confidence may bind,
And make them follow at your call
 If you are always kind.
      —*Sarah Josepha Hale.* *

Sequel to an Old Story: Mary's Lamb

Mary had a little lamb,
 Which grew to be a sheep;
The wool upon its back became
 Too thick and warm to keep.

Then Mary's sheep did with the rest
 Down to the brookside go,
And soon again it well could boast
 "A fleece as white as snow."

The shearer came, and with his shears
 Cut off the heavy wool,
Till every sheep was shorn at last
 And all the bags were full.

*Poems for Our Children, *1830.*

The wool that came from Mary's sheep
    Was spun and woven, dears,
And made into a nice warm coat
    That Mary wore for years!
            — *Emilie Poulsson.* *

The Owl and the Pussy-Cat

The Owl and the Pussy-cat went to sea
    In a beautiful pea-green boat,
They took some honey, and plenty of money,
    Wrapped up in a five-pound note.
The Owl looked up to the stars above,
    And sang to a small guitar,
'O lovely Pussy! 'O Pussy, my love,
    What a beautiful Pussy you are,
        You are,
        You are!
What a beautiful Pussy you are!'

Pussy said to the Owl, 'You elegant fowl!
    How charmingly sweet you sing!
O let us be married! Too long we have tarried;
    But what shall we do for a ring?'
They sailed away, for a year and a day,
    To the land where the Bong-tree grows
And there in a wood a Piggy-wig stood
    With a ring at the end of his nose,
        His nose,
        His nose,
    With a ring at the end of his nose.

'Dear Pig, are you willing to sell for one shilling
    Your ring?' Said the Piggy, 'I will.'
So they took it away, and were married next day
    By the Turkey who lives on the hill.
They dined on mince, and slices of quince,
    Which they ate with a runcible spoon;
And hand in hand, on the edge of the sand,
    They danced by the light of the moon,
        The moon,
        The moon,
They danced by the light of the moon.
            — *Edward Lear.*

*In the Child's World, *1893*.

The Nutcrackers and the Sugar-Tongs

The Nutcrackers sat by a plate on the table,
    The Sugar-tongs sat by a plate at his side;
And the Nutcrackers said, "Don't you wish we were able
    Along the blue hills and green meadows to ride?
Must we drag on this stupid existence for ever,
    So idle and weary, so full of remorse, —
While every one else takes his pleasure, and never
    Seems happy unless he is riding a horse?

"Don't you think we could ride without being instructed?
    Without any saddle, or bridle, or spur?
Our legs are so long, and so aptly constructed,
    I'm sure that an accident could not occur.
Let us all of a sudden hop down from the table,
    And hustle downstairs, and each jump on a horse!
Shall we try? Shall we go? Do you think we are able?"
    The Sugar-tongs answered distinctly, "Of course!"

So down the long staircase they hopped in a minute,
    The Sugar-tongs snapped, and the Crackers said
        "crack!"
The stable was open, the horses were in it;
    Each took out a pony, and jumped on his back.
The Cat in a fright scrambled out of the doorway,
    The Mice tumbled out of a bundle of hay,
The brown and white Rats, and the black ones from
    Norway,
    Screamed out, "They are taking the horses away!"

The whole of the household was filled with amazement,
    The Cups and the Saucers danced madly about,
The Plates and the Dishes looked out of the casement,
    The Saltcellar stood on his head with a shout,
The Spoons with a clatter looked out of the lattice,
    The Mustard-pot climbed up the Gooseberry Pies,
The Soup-ladle peeped through a heap of Veal Patties,
    And squeaked with a ladle-like scream of surprise.

The Frying-pan said, "It's an awful delusion!"
    The Tea-kettle hissed and grew black in the face;
And they all rushed downstairs in the wildest confusion,
    To see the great Nutcracker-Sugar-tong race.
And out of the stable, with screamings and laughter,

(Their ponies were cream-coloured, speckled with
    brown,)
The Nutcrackers first, and the Sugar-tongs after,
    Rode all round the yard, and then all round the town.

They rode through the street, and they rode by the station,
    They galloped away to the beautiful shore;
In silence they rode, and made no observation,
    Save this: "We will never go back any more!"
And still you might hear, till they rode out of hearing,
    The Sugar-tongs snap, and the Crackers say "crack!"
Till far in the distance their forms disappearing,
    They faded away. — And they never came back!
                 — *Edward Lear.*

Fable: The Mountain and the Squirrel

The mountain and the squirrel
Had a quarrel,
And the former called the latter "Little Prig";
Bun replied,
"You are doubtless very big;
But all sorts of things and weather
Must be taken in together,
To make up a year
And a sphere.
And I think it no disgrace
To occupy my place.
If I'm not so large as you,
You are not so small as I,
And not half so spry.
I'll not deny you make
A very pretty squirrel track;
Talents differ; all is well and wisely put;
If I cannot carry forests on my back,
Neither can you crack a nut."
               — *Ralph Waldo Emerson.*

The Blind Men and the Elephant

It was six men of Indostan
    To learning much inclined,

Who went to see the elephant
    (Though all of them were blind),
That each by observation
    Might satisfy his mind.

The First approached the elephant,
    And, happening to fall
Against his broad and sturdy side,
    At once began to bawl:
"God bless me! but the elephant
    Is nothing but a wall!"

The Second, feeling of the tusk,
    Cried: "Ho! what have we here
So very round and smooth and sharp?
    To me 'tis mighty clear
This wonder of an elephant
    Is very like a spear!"

The Third approached the animal,
    And, happening to take
The squirming trunk within his hands,
    Thus boldly up and spake:
"I see," quoth he, "the elephant
    Is very like a snake!"

The Fourth reached out his eager hand,
    And felt about the knee:
"What most this wondrous beast is like
    Is might plain," quoth he;
"'Tis clear enough the elephant
    Is very like a tree."

The Fifth, who chanced to touch the ear,
    Said: "E'en the blindest man
Can tell what this resembles most;
    Deny the fact who can,
This marvel of an elephant
    Is very like a fan!"

The Sixth no sooner had begun
    About the beast to grope,
Than, seizing on the swinging tail
    That fell within his scope,
"I see," quoth he, "the elephant
    Is very like a rope!"

And so these men of Indostan
   Disputed loud and long,
Each in his own opinion
   Exceeding stiff and strong,
Though each was partly in the right,
   And all were in the wrong!

So, oft in the theologic wars
   The disputants, I ween,
Rail on in utter ignorance
   Of what each other mean,
And prate about an elephant
   Not one of them has seen!
              —*John Godfrey Saxe.**

The Walrus and the Carpenter

The sun was shining on the sea,
   Shining with all his might;
He did his very best to make
   The billows smooth and bright —
And this was odd, because it was
   The middle of the night.

The moon was shining sulkily,
   Because she thought the sun
Had got no business to be there
   After the day was done —
"It's very rude of him," she said,
   "To come and spoil the fun!"

The sea was wet as wet could be,
   The sands were dry as dry.
You could not see a cloud, because
   No cloud was in the sky;
No birds were flying overhead —
   There were no birds to fly.

The Walrus and the Carpenter
   Were walking close at hand;
They wept like anything to see
   Such quantities of sand —
"If this were only cleared away,"
   They said, "it would be grand!"

"If seven maids with seven mops
   Swept it for half a year,
Do you suppose," the Walrus said,
   "That they could get it clear?"
"I doubt it," said the Carpenter,
   And shed a bitter tear.

"O Oysters, come and walk with us!"
   The Walrus did beseech.
"A pleasant walk, a pleasant talk,
   Along the briny beach;
We cannot do with more than four,
   To give a hand to each."

The eldest Oyster looked at him,
   But never a word he said;
The eldest Oyster winked his eye,
   And shook his heavy head —
Meaning to say he did not choose
   To leave the oyster-bed.

But four young Oysters hurried up,
   All eager for the treat;
Their coats were brushed, their
     faces washed,
   Their shoes were clean and neat —
And this was odd, because, you know,
   They hadn't any feet.

*Poems, *1850.*

Four other Oysters followed them,
  And yet another four;
And thick and fast they came at last,
  And more, and more, and more —
All hopping through the frothy waves,
  And scrambling to the shore.

The Walrus and the Carpenter
  Walked on a mile or so,
And then they rested on a rock
  Conveniently low —
And all the little Oysters stood
  And waited in a row.

"The time has come," the Walrus said,
  "To talk of many things:
Of shoes–and ships–and sealing wax–
  Of cabbages — and kings —
And why the sea is boiling hot —
  And whether pigs have wings."

"But wait a bit," the Oysters cried,
  "Before we have our chat;
For some of us are out of breath,
  And all of us are fat!"
"No hurry!" said the Carpenter.
  They thanked him much for that.

"A loaf of bread," the Walrus said,
  "Is what we chiefly need;
Pepper and vinegar besides
  Are very good indeed —
Now, if you're ready, Oysters dear,
  We can begin to feed."

"But not on us!" the Oysters cried,
  Turning a little blue.
"After such kindness, that would be
  A dismal thing to do!"
"The night is fine," the Walrus said.
  "Do you admire the view?"

"It was so kind of you to come!
  And you are very nice!"
The Carpenter said nothing, but,
  "Cut us another slice.
I wish you were not quite so deaf —
  "I've had to ask you twice!"

"It seems a shame," the Walrus said,
  "To play them such a trick.
After we've brought them out so far,
  And made them trot so quick!"
The Carpenter said nothing but,
  "The butter's spread too thick!"

"I weep for you," the Walrus said;
  "I deeply sympathize."
With sobs and tears he sorted out
  Those of the largest size,
Holding his pocket-handkerchief
  Before his streaming eyes.

"O Oysters," said the Carpenter,
  "You've had a pleasant run!
Shall we be trotting home again?"
  But answer came there none —
And this was scarcely odd, because
  They'd eaten every one.
          — *Lewis Carroll.*

Jabberwocky

'Twas brillig, and the slithy toves
  Did gyre and gimble in the wabe:
All mimsy were the borogoves,
  And the mome raths outgrabe.

"Beware the Jabberwock, my son!
  The jaws that bite, the claws that catch!

Beware the Jubjub bird, and shun
  The frumious Bandersnatch!"

He took his vorpal sword in hand:
  Long time the manxome foe he sought —
So rested he by the Tumtum tree,
  And stood awhile in thought.

And, as in uffish thought he stood,
  The Jabberwock with eyes of flame,
Came whiffling through the tulgey wood,
  And burbled as it came!

One, two! One, two! And through and through
  The vorpal blade went snicker-snack!
He left it dead, and with its head
  He went galumphing back.

"And hast thou slain the Jabberwock?
  Come to my arms, my beamish boy!
O frabjous day! Callooh! Callay!"
  He chortled in his joy.

'Twas brillig, and the slithy toves
  Did gyre and gimble in the wabe:
All mimsy were the borogoves,
  And the mome raths outgrabe.
                                    — *Lewis Carroll*.

The Little Land

When at home alone I sit,
And am very tired of it,
I have just to shut my eyes
To go sailing through the skies —
To go sailing far away
To the pleasant Land of Play;
To the fairy land afar
Where the Little People are;
Where the clover-tops are trees,
And the rain-pools are the seas,
And the leaves, like little ships,
Sail about on tiny trips;
And above the daisy tree
  Through the grasses,

High o'erhead the Bumble Bee
  Hums and passes.

In that forest to and fro
I can wander, I can go;
See the spider and the fly,
And the ants go marching by,
Carrying parcels with their feet
Down the green and grassy street.
I can in the sorrel sit
Where the ladybird alit.
I can climb the jointed grass
  And on high
See the greater swallows pass

In the sky,
And the round sun rolling by
Heeding no such things as I.

Through that forest I can pass
Till, as in a looking-glass,
Humming fly and daisy tree
And my tiny self I see,
Painted very clear and neat
On the rain-pool at my feet.
Should a leaflet come to land
Drifting near to where I stand,
Straight I'll board that tiny boat
Round the rain-pool sea to float.
Little thoughtful creatures sit
On the grassy coasts of it;
Little things with lovely eyes
See me sailing with surprise.
Some are clad in armour green —
(These have sure to battle been!) —

Some are pied with ev'ry hue,
Black and crimson, gold and blue;
Some have wings and swift are
    gone; —
But they all look kindly on.

When my eyes I once again
    Open, and see all things plain:
High bare walls, great bare floor;
Great big knobs on drawer and door;
Great big people perched on chairs,
Stitching tucks and mending tears,
Each a hill that I could climb,
And talking nonsense all the time —
    O dear me,
    That I could be
A sailor on the rain-pool sea,
A climber in the clover tree,
And just come back, a sleepy-head,
Late at night to go to bed.
    — *Robert Louis Stevenson.* *

The Duel

The gingham dog and the calico cat
Side by side on the table sat;
'Twas half-past twelve, and (what do you think!)
Nor one nor t'other had slept a wink!
The old Dutch clock and the Chinese plate
Appeared to know as sure as fate
There was going to be a terrible spat.
(I wasn't there, I simply state
What was told to me by the Chinese plate!)

The gingham dog went "bow-wow-wow!"
And the calico cat replied "mee-ow!"
The air was littered, an hour or so,
With bits of gingham and calico,
While the old Dutch clock in the chimney-place
Up with its hands before its face,
For it always dreaded a family row!
(Now mind: I'm only telling you
What the old Dutch clock declares is true!)

*A Child's Garden of Verses, 1885.

The Chinese plate looked very blue.
And wailed, "Oh dear! what shall we do!"
But the gingham dog and the calico cat
Wallowed this way and tumbled that,
Employing every tooth and claw
In the awfullest way you ever saw —
And, oh! how the gingham and calico flew!
(Don't fancy I exaggerate!
I got my news from the Chinese plate!)

Next morning, where the two had sat,
They found no trace of dog or cat;
And some folks think unto this day
That burglars stole that pair away!
But the truth about the cat and pup
Is this: they ate each other up!
Now what do you really think of that!
(The old Dutch clock it told me so,
And that is how I came to know.)
— *Eugene Field.* *

The Sugar-Plum Tree

Have you ever heard of the Sugar-Plum Tree?
    'Tis a marvel of great renown!
It blooms on the shore of the Lollypop Sea
    In the garden of Shut-Eye Town;
The fruit that it bears is so wondrously sweet
    (As those who have tasted it say)
That good little children have only to eat
    Of that fruit to be happy next day.

When you've got to the tree, you would have
    a hard time
    To capture the fruit which I sing;
The tree is so tall that no person could climb
    To the boughs where the sugar-plums swing!
But up in that tree sits a chocolate cat,
    And a gingerbread dog prowls below —
And this is the way you contrive to get at
    Those sugar-plums tempting you so:

*Lullabyland, *1892.

You say but the word to that gingerbread dog
    And he barks with such terrible zest
That the chocolate cat is at once all agog,
    As her swelling proportions attest.
And the chocolate cat goes cavorting around
    From this leafy limb unto that,
And the sugar-plums tumble, of course, to the ground —
    Hurrah for that chocolate cat!

There are marshmallows, gumdrops, and peppermint
    canes
    With stripings of scarlet or gold,
And you carry away of the treasure that rains,
    As much as your apron can hold!
So come, little child, cuddle closer to me
    In your dainty white nightcap and gown,
And I'll rock you away to that Sugar-Plum Tree
    In the garden of Shut-Eye Town.
                  — *Eugene Field.* *

Santa Claus and the Mouse

One Christmas eve, when Santa Claus
    Came to a certain house,
To fill the children's stockings there,
    He found a little mouse.

"A merry Christmas, little friend,"
    Said Santa, good and kind.
"The same to you, sir," said the mouse;
    "I thought you wouldn't mind.

"If I should stay awake to-night
    And watch you for awhile."
"You're very welcome, little mouse,"
    Said Santa, with a smile.

And then he filled the stockings up
    Before the mouse could wink —
From toe to top, from top to toe,
    There wasn't left a chink.

*Lullabyland, *1892*.

"Now, they won't hold another thing,"
    Said Santa Claus, with pride.
A twinkle came in mouse's eyes,
    But humbly he replied:

"It's not polite to contradict —
    Your pardon I implore —
But in the fullest stocking there
    I could put one thing more."

"Oh, ho!" laughed Santa, "silly mouse.
    Don't I know how to pack?
By filling stockings all these years,
    I should have learned the knack."

And then he took the stocking down
    From where it hung so high,
And said: "Now put in one thing more;
    I give you leave to try."

The mousie chuckled to himself,
    And then he softly stole
Right to the stocking's crowded toe
    And gnawed a little hole!

"Now, if you please, good Santa Claus,
    I've put in one thing more;
For you will own that little hole
    Was not in there before."

How Santa Claus did laugh and laugh!
    And then he gayly spoke:
"Well! you shall have a Christmas cheese
    For that nice little joke."

If you don't think this story true,
    Why! I can show to you
The very stocking with the hole
    The little mouse gnawed through.
                — *Emilie Poulsson.* *

*In the Child's World, *1893.

A Visit from St. Nicholas

'Twas the night before Christmas, when all through
    the house
Not a creature was stirring, not even a mouse.
The stockings were hung by the chimney with care,
In hopes that St. Nicholas soon would be there.
The children were nestled all snug in their beds,
While visions of sugar-plums danced in their heads;
And mama in her kerchief, and I in my cap,
Had just settled our brains for a long winter's nap —
When out on the lawn there arose such a clatter
I sprang from my bed to see what was the matter.
Away to the window I flew like a flash,
Tore open the shutter, and threw up the sash.
The moon on the breast of the new-fallen snow
Gave a lustre of midday to objects below;
When what to my wondering eyes should appear
But a miniature sleigh and eight tiny reindeer,
With a little old driver, so lively and quick,
I knew in a moment it must be St. Nick!
More rapid than eagles his coursers they came,
And he whistled and shouted and called them by name.
"Now, Dasher! now, Dancer! now, Prancer and Vixen!
On, Comet! on, Cupid! on Donner and Blitzen! —
To the top of the porch, to the top of the wall,
Now, dash away, dash away, dash away all!"
As dry leaves that before the wild hurricane fly,
When they meet with an obstacle mount to the sky,
So, up to the housetop the coursers they flew,
With a sleigh full of toys — and St. Nicholas, too.
And then, in a twinkling, I heard on the roof
The prancing and pawing of each little hoof.
As I drew in my head, and was turning around,
Down the chimney St. Nicholas came with a bound:
He was dressed all in fur from his head to his foot,
And his clothes were all tarnished with ashes and soot:
A bundle of toys he had flung on his back,
And he looked like a peddler just opening his pack.
His eyes, how they twinkled! his dimples, how merry!
His cheeks were like roses, his nose like a cherry;
His droll little mouth was drawn up like a bow,
And the beard on his chin was as white as the snow.
The stump of a pipe he held tight in his teeth,
And the smoke, it encircled his head like a wreath.

He had a broad face and a little round belly
That shook, when he laughed, like a bowl full of jelly.
He was chubby and plump — a right jolly old elf;
And I laughed when I saw him, in spite of myself;
A wink of his eye, and a twist of his head,
Soon gave me to know I had nothing to dread.
He spoke not a word, but went straight to his work,
And filled all the stockings: then turned with a jerk,
And laying his finger aside of his nose,
And giving a nod, up the chimney he rose.
He sprang to his sleigh, to his team gave a whistle,
And away they all flew like the down of a thistle.
But I heard him exclaim, ere they drove out of sight,
"Happy Christmas to all, and to all a goodnight!"
                                        — *Clement C. Moore.**

*Sentinal, *Troy, New York, 1823.*

Index

Titles, "First lines," Authors' Names, SELECTED SUBJECTS

T

U

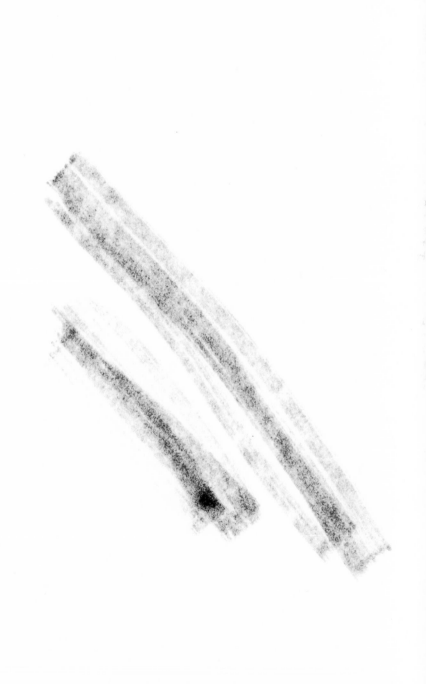